## Chapter 1

## Help I Am Drowning!

The drip is what got me. That steady drip, drip, drip. I could have taken the rush of a gush of life but that steady drip, drip of life began to wear away at my soul. At first I really didn't notice that the waters of life were rising. After all, the days rolled by so quickly. Then one day I looked around and the waters were up to my nose hairs.

How did it happen? Who was watching for me? Why didn't I see this? Why didn't somebody warn me? It's too late! I was drowning. I was drowning on dry earth, but I could not get my footing. With one last attempt to get out of my premature watery grave, I pushed up and cried for help. A hand reached down for me and began to pull me from the water bath. About half way out of the watery grave that now had become for me a warm bath, I realized that I was freezing.

Let me go, let me go I screamed!

But you will drown. The water is continuing to rise.

No, No I am freezing and the water is so warm.

I wiggled and wiggled until the firm grasp of rescue was forced to let go. Back into the warm water I dropped only to find that I could not touch the bottom. I could not swim. One of the last sounds I heard before waking up on dry ground was the gurgle of a drain. Recovery began.

When life's hardest issues begin they are almost manageable. But as they continue to manifest in your life the steady drip, one thing after another, begins to form that watery grave.

Depression feels like you are drowning. Addiction draws you into the watery grave. Divorce, cancer, loss of a loved one, loss of a job, along with other major life issues suck a person into a deep dark abyss of despair. What happens to a person who has struggled through a hard life event and finds that all of their boundaries are destroyed? What happens when the defense system of life has gapping wounds?

Recovery begins at that moment, it does not end there. So often after the hospital stay, after the recovery house, or after the divorce, friends and family expect you to put on a happy face and go on with life. But what life do you go on with? The old one is over and the new one is not yet come.

The story of Nehemiah is a story that sheds light on what a person must do to be restored. The story in the Bible speaks of a city being restored but really it was about life being restored. The city was restored to a sustainable life. The boundaries were rebuilt with new material so that safety became familiar. It is through the eyes of the restoration of Jerusalem that many have found the strength to rebuild a safe life which is sustainable and powerful..

This book is about restoring a life that has been in the watery grave of depression, addiction, divorce, etc. This plan that Nehemiah used so long ago still works today for recovery and restoration.

# Chapter 2

# Nehemiah Gives An Allegory

Looking at Nehemiah's life and the work he did to help restore Jerusalem shows the need for secure boundaries in our lives. At each section of wall and each gate we will see the need for restoring the boundaries addiction has destroyed. The gates and walls of our lives are the strongest defense against relapse and defeat.

In the study of Nehemiah the pattern for recovery can be used for more than just the walls of the city. Nehemiah rebuilt the twelve life gates as well as the city gates for the people of Jerusalem. The twelve life gates which should be rebuilt through recovery are reality, authority, a belief system based on truth, self-esteem based on biblical morals, trust, empowerment, freedom, a future, relationships, a new harvest, and a sense of belonging and joy.

Addiction and other debilitating issues rob us of our strength, the ability to make healthy choices and the ability to say no to destructive behaviors. Each gate in Nehemiah will support an area of our lives which must be rebuilt and protected. As with a city that is well protected, restoring the gates and walls of our lives will provide a safe haven for a healthy environment for living a godly life.

During the study of the gates and the rebuilding of the correlated gates of our lives we will have the opportunity to rebuild self-esteem and regain self-respect. We will be restored to God, to ourselves, to others and to the community as the gates of our lives are re-established.

Just as the gates were rebuilt and maintained, the walls and gates have to be maintained for life or the enemy will soon find entry into the inner safety of the city. We may discover and even rebuild the gates and walls in a short period of time but they must be maintained for life. In some of our lives, the gates themselves will take years to rebuild. We may be like the people who lived in Jerusalem for many years struggling with robbers attacking the city at night because the walls were not reconstructed.

Like a person who wishes to try to get sober or the person trying to overcome depression without rebuilding his or her life boundaries, the enemy quickly finds a way to destroy everything he or she may think she has gained. Over and over we may struggle to keep what we have when the boundaries are not in place. Over and over we will find ourselves disappointed with our progress unless we take a long look at the boundaries of our lives and begin to rebuild the walls of security.

**Proverbs 25:28, "He that hath no rule over his own spirit is like a city that is broken down, and without walls."** (KJV) Nehemiah gives us the formula for taking control over our spirit and restoring our lives to what God had originally intended.

*It should be noted here that these gates may not be in the order recorded in the book of Nehemiah. However, all the gates are connected in a line to form the wall. All the gates and walls were being reconstructed at the same time; therefore these gates may or may not follow in order with the book of Nehemiah. Also, some disagreement exists as to the number of actual gates rebuilt in the book of Nehemiah. I do not wish to contend with those who say there are only ten gates mentioned. My study is based on personal revelation backed up by years of personal study and experience.*

The Valley Gate is next to the Old Gate and the Dung Gate. As we look at the construction of these gates we find that the foundational beliefs in God and the reality of God are very connected to the rebuilding of relationships at the Dung Gate and the Fish Gates. If we start at the Sheep Gate, as does the book of Nehemiah, we can see the connection of community to relationships. Relationship rebuilding is connected to the rebuilding of our beliefs in God. Relationship rebuilding is definitely connected to the rebuilding of self. Self-esteem goes a long way to rebuilding our community attachments. Empowerment is connected to the authority of God and to restoring relationships and relationships to self.

For the sake of our study we will look at all the gates that pertain to restoring our relationship to God first; then the gates that restore self, followed by the gates that restore relationships to others and finally the gates that restore our relationship to our community.

The problem with hard issues of life is that they affect all parts of a person. Take for example financial problems. The financial problem, though of a material nature, affects the physical, the spiritual and the emotional or soul state of a man or woman. Just recently I spoke with a young person who said money was the issue. When the issue was out of hand, his emotions got out of hand. He was also having trouble spiritually because he could not understand why God would let these things happen to him. The problem affected his entire world. Addiction is the same. It may be a drug or alcohol that presents as the problem but the issue goes much deeper. Recovery starts with three words, "I need help."

# Chapter 3

# Nehemiah's Story

Nehemiah was, according to scriptures, a cupbearer to the king. He was in a pretty comfortable job as long as no one was trying to assassinate the king. He was at the side of the king for every meal, every snack, and every drink of water for nothing touched the lips of the king without Nehemiah tasting it first. In the context of our society today here is a man with a good job, nice house, well behaved children and a place of significance and position. He had arrived, as we say. He was comfortable and surrounded by elegance and sophistication, yet Nehemiah was haunted by the conditions of his people. This comfortable Jew in exile had family in Jerusalem who were trying to rebuild a city completely destroyed and ravished and he was curious to know what was going on in Jerusalem.

One day his curiosity got the best of him and he asked a message bearer how things were going. Nehemiah was surprised to hear that things were not going so well. The message bearer told Nehemiah that the workers were discouraged because the progress was slow. It seemed that each time the workers rebuilt parts of the city enemies would run through the walls and take anything and everything leaving the workers to constantly build and rebuild.

The temple was not yet finished due to the discouragement of the workers and the fact that they felt they had to protect their own families by fortifying their own homes. Nehemiah was concerned and took the matter to prayer. While in prayer the Lord laid out a plan to Nehemiah to go to Jerusalem and help his people. Feeling the urgency to do something, Nehemiah was quite overtaken with responsibility as well as fear for what the king might do to him if he would take a leave of absence. The Bible says that Nehemiah's countenance was heavy and the king asked him to explain his mood. Nehemiah at once told the king about his desire to help his people and the rest is history. Nehemiah left with money and provisions from the king to begin the work of restoring the walls of Jerusalem.

**Nehemiah 1:3, "and they said to me, 'The remnant who are left of the captivity and were in the province are in great affliction and reproach' the wall of Jerusalem is broken down, and its gates are burned with fire.'"**

When Nehemiah asked one of "the brethren" about Jerusalem he was told disturbing news. He was told that the remnant who had left the captivity of Babylon and started the work of rebuilding their lives in Jerusalem were in trouble. These people who had left Babylon with Ezra for the purpose of building a city, a home, and a life in their hometown were greatly "afflicted and in reproach."

What Nehemiah did is what every minister called to help the afflicted and those who are in reproach would do. He sat down and wept. He mourned the need of the people in Jerusalem. Nehemiah was so torn by the news of the oppression of his people that he fasted and prayed. In verse five of chapter one Nehemiah appeals to God for help based on God's great mercy and covenant keeping promises. Nehemiah confesses his sin and the sin of those in trouble in Jerusalem. He admits that he and the others have dealt treacherously against God. In verse nine Nehemiah reminds God that if the people return to Him that He would redeem them and return them to their homeland. Nehemiah reminds God of His promise to restore. He reminds God that these people are the ones God has redeemed and that they need His help. Nehemiah not only asks God for help for the people but asks God to give him favor with the king so he can go to Jerusalem to help in the restoration.

Throughout the book of Nehemiah we can see that this man of God was not ashamed to ask for help. More than once Nehemiah asked for help. He admitted this problem is too big for him to handle alone. From day one, Nehemiah sought God to direct his journey to restoration and recovery.

When Nehemiah found favor with the king to go to Jerusalem for a visit and to take supplies in order to help the people rebuild the walls, he was not without opposition. As soon as those who had opposed the people in Jerusalem heard that Nehemiah was coming to help, they began at once to cause him trouble.

Sanballat and Tobiah represent the opposition that exists to any recovery plan. You can call this the devil, or addiction, or co-dependency or any number of other names, but nevertheless it is opposition to recovery. This opposition will be present from the first moment the plan for recovery is set in place. Call them the naysayers. These are those people who say, "you can't change," and "There is no way you can ever get sober and stay sober."

So often the problem makers in the life of recovery are people you would never expect to cause you problems. They are family members, close friends, and co-workers. These people are never thinking that they would stop you from recovery. They are the ones who "just are telling you how it is." Such was the way of Sanballat and Tobiah. They were greatly "grieved" because Nehemiah had come to seek the welfare of the children of Israel. Nehemiah had to prepare himself for what was to come from the opposition. Sanballat and Tobiah were in leadership in the provinces around Jerusalem. They hated the Jews. They did not want the Israelites to succeed. In the recovery process, or let us call it the change process, there will be people who do not want you to succeed. They may not want to make changes themselves, or they may just want you to continue to support what they are doing, or many other reasons. Your success will not be important to them.

This is what Nehemiah did as he arrived in Jerusalem. First, he told only a select few what God had put in his heart. So often we get too excited, too puffed up and start making claims and promises before we ever know that the job of restoration will take. Nehemiah held his tongue so he would not give the enemies any ammunition.

Quietly Nehemiah surveyed the problem. This indicates he had sound judgment about making a plan. He counted the cost. He took a look at just how bad the problem was before he made any suggestions as to how to get the job done. Nehemiah had, from the beginning, shown restraint in his character and he has shown strength as he has waited on God to show him exactly what should be done.

Next, Nehemiah went to the worst sites for reconstruction first. He went and assessed the Valley Gate and the Dung Gate of the city. It is thought that at the Valley Gate was the Hinnon Valley. Remember Nehemiah prayed that the Israelites had abandoned the promises of God and had treated God badly.

The Valley Gate was on the west side of the city and opened to the Hinnon Valley. The Israelites were notorious for idol worship. It was at the valley of Hinnon that history reveals the sacrifice of children of Israel to the god Molech. Molech was said to be idolized as a brazen statute of a "man/beast" that held his arms out to receive the sacrifices of children. Priests of the brazen "altar" would heat the statue to unbelievably high temperatures and the children would be "roasted" in the arms of the pagan god Molech.

Hinnon was also known as the Valley of Gehenna which Jesus referred to in the New Testament as the eternal fire or hell. **Mark 9:43, "If your hand causes you to sin, cut it off. It is better for you to enter life maimed than with two hands to go into hell, where the fire never goes out."**

Nehemiah looked at the destruction of the gates of the Valley and the Dung Gate. It is interesting that these gates led into the Hinnon Valley where the Israelites made the most mockery of the love of God by sacrificing their children to the god Molech. It is no wonder God called for the destruction of Jerusalem. Nehemiah saw the destruction and the devastation of the city by examining the worst part of the destruction first. He began the journey to recovery where the people demonstrated the most disrespect for God.

As we start our recovery process, we too must start at the lowest part of our lives. We will never begin recovery on the "top." Recovery and change will only come after all the other doors are closed and we are at our lowest place for recovery. Restoration begins with looking at where we are and where we want to be. In the book of Nehemiah we are told that he put together a team of people to help him rebuild the walls and especially the gates of Jerusalem.

The gates of each city were specific entrances for different parts of city life. The name of the gate related to the activities that occurred at that gate. The people who helped to rebuild that section and gate directly benefited from the restoration. Likewise, as you rebuild your life, there are specific areas where ideas, people, and dreams can enter. You will rebuild boundaries with the help of people who are involved in your life at the gate.

Recovery will be putting together a team of people who are headed in the same direction you are and who will not tear you down or cause you to stumble, those who will hold you accountable as you make the way to a new lifestyle.

## Chapter 4

## The Gates Restored

The first gate that you will find destroyed is the Valley Gate. Nehemiah began his inspection of the city of Jerusalem at the Valley Gate. On horseback, Nehemiah saw the great devastation of the gate at the lowest portion of the city. As he looked at the despair he knew the work would be consuming. He knew that this could not be accomplished in his power alone, but that the people who lived in despair must garner enough strength to restore their own lives. He would lead them and work beside them, but they must work as well.

You will learn to say "I need help" at the Valley Gate. You will learn to admit the problem. You will learn to access what the reality of the problem is and begin to explain to yourself and others what the problem is at the Valley Gate. Also at the Valley Gate you will begin to choose forgiveness. Forgiveness is a process but it is also a command of Jesus. He says in Matthew that unless you forgive your brother that God will not forgive you. **Matthew 6:14-15, "For if you forgive men their trespasses, your heavenly Father will also forgive you. But if you do not forgive men their trespasses, neither will your Father forgive your trespasses."**

The East Gate is the gateway to restoring authority. You will learn that God can help but you must commit.

You will also learn to choose love at the East Gate. Authority on every level is destroyed by addiction and other life issues. We give up our own authority, we refuse authority and we reject authority which can help us. The restoration of authority in our lives helps us to accept the leadership of God and others. It is at the East Gate that authority is the strongest. The Bible speaks of Jesus returning and coming in the East. When Jesus returns, His authority will be completely restored and He will be the victor over all evil. When authority is restored in our lives we are able to respect God's authority to restore sanity in our lives. We also learn to respect the authority that God has given to others over us.

At the Old Gate truth is restored. It is at the gate of ancient beginnings that truths are restored to us. You will learn to believe in the truths of God's word, learn that you can submit to those truths and choose the hope of the truth of the Word of God.

It has been in the beginnings of our lives that we have chosen to believe the lies of the devil. We have believed that change is impossible for us, we have believed we are worthless and that others are out to get us. Once truth is restored, the lies will drop away opening up the way for replacing the broken down boundaries with strong beliefs about God, about ourselves, about others and about the communities we live in. You will learn to pray to God about the traditions of men. You will begin to learn about what traditions are worth keeping and those which are not.

The Inspection Gate is the gateway to restoring self. At this gate you will learn that you can look at yourself, that you can take responsibility and that you can choose self-control.

So much of the time we fail to look at ourselves in a realistic way. As you can see, by the time you get to the gate of inspection, you have already rebuilt the Valley Gate, the East Gate and the Old Gate. In these places are boundaries for asking for help, admitting the problem, restoring authority, and replacing false beliefs with the truth. After those gates are restored you will have the courage to really look at yourself in new way.

At the Fountain Gate trust will be rebuilt. Trust is so often destroyed by addiction. We cannot trust others or ourselves. At this gate you will learn that you can tell your story to another. You will learn to remember your life as it really was and choose to be vulnerable. It will take additional courage to choose vulnerability, but as the other gates are restored, the choice will be a little easier.

It is at the Horse Gate that empowerment is restored. Once empowerment is restored you will find that you can change, you can choose and you can do the right thing. Empowerment implies strength of character, trust and resources. At this gate you will begin to recognize faithfulness and steadfastness in your character being formed.

The Prison Gate is the gateway to restoring freedom. Here you will learn to walk away a free person. You will learn to move forward and begin to declare that you are free. It is only when we have been imprisoned that we can truly know what freedom is. But with freedom comes work.  Freedom is a new way of life.  It is walking away from the things that have bound us and enslaved us.  In freedom we must learn new skills and concentrate on new things.

The Dung Gate is the gateway to restoring our future.  Here we learn that we can dig up, let go and rebuild.  It was at the Dung Gate that Nehemiah realized the devastation of the city but it was also at the Dung Gate that he decided that there could be a future for Jerusalem.

The Fish Gate restores relationships.  There you will learn to give, to love and to live.  Jesus told his disciples that they would be fishers of men.  We must set new boundaries in our relationships by giving of ourselves, learning about what real love is and that love is meant to be.

The Vendor Gate restores a new harvest.  After sowing seeds of evil and destruction and reaping much of that harvest through addiction, we must learn to sow good seeds.  It is here we will learn to do good deeds, to build a good work ethic and to sow by giving to the things of God.

The Sheep Gate is the gate of restoring belonging in our lives.  Addiction and life issues steal our sense of belonging.  We have no place, we often say.  It is here we will begin to learn that we are in the body of Christ and in a new family.  It is in this family that we will learn to serve and know that we belong.

Finally, at the Water Gate our joy will be restored.  When joy is restored to our lives, we can speak of that joy, we can share of that joy and we can celebrate the new life in Christ.

The Twelve Gates of Recovery and Restoration are designed to be helpful to all you suffer from the agonies of life. Addiction is such a stigmatized life. It has so many stereotypes that depict people as bums and criminals of little or no worth. Addiction covers a wide array of life problems. The definition of addition covers any habitual problem that can be stopped by an individual. Using this definition I have discovered many habitual problems which people need help to overcome.

The Twelve Gates of Recovery and Restoration are not designed to be worked alone. Although the work lends itself to self-evaluation, we believe that it is through small groups that the best results are achieved. It is through accountability and reliability that change is accomplished. Accountability to others is like a rubber band; it stretches to allow freedom but holds to require change. Reliability is the idea of trust earned through faithfulness. In reliability we learn the character traits of faithfulness and truthfulness working in conjunction with mercy and grace.

## Chapter 5

## How Small Groups Work

Small groups are designed for accountability. Each small group should have a meeting to define the level of accountability it will have. At a recovery group the highest level of accountability is expected. At this level group participants must choose to "join." There should be an expectation of confrontation in a loving manner. Questions should be expected to be answered. What happens in the group must stay in the group as long as what is happening is positive and good.

Accountability could require sign ins and follow ups. It should require untruths to be addressed. Confronting in a group should always be respectful and done in love that lifts and does not destroy.

Guilt and shame should be avoided in small groups. Acceptance and compassion should always employ ways to stop the negative behavior. Advice should be avoided but facts and biblical wisdom should be available.

Reliability of the time, dates, and meeting places are a must for the group to work. Reliability and faithfulness of the leader is necessary for the group to work. When a person is not faithful to the meetings this could be an indication that the person is struggling.

I recommend a partner for each member of the group. One of the partners must be stable in their life issues to help the other partner. The leader of the group should also hold the partners accountable for growth. If there is no visible growth in the partnership, the leader may have to suggest new partnerships.

These partnerships should be held to strict boundaries. There should be no male female partnerships unless they are married to each other. There should be no female partnerships where gender issues are evident. There should be no male partnerships where gender issues are evident.

One of the reasons the twelve gates have been so successful is the family atmosphere and comradeship the program enjoys.

Some of the core teachings of the twelve gates are taught by lifestyle. Leaders of the groups should be restored themselves. We feel that our life issues are restored in layers. Our boundaries are restored by the walls that we build one level at a time.

## How Reliability Enhances Restoration

The Twelve Gates of Recovery and Restoration are built on the foundation of family and community. It is in relationships that we are wounded and hurt. It is in communities that trust is often destroyed and relationships relinquished to loneliness and disillusionment. Logic may suggest that healing comes in isolation but healing comes in restored families and solid communities. As you will notice Nehemiah used family groups to rebuild each section of the walls and gates and the whole community came together to build the whole wall. In the end the family groups were connected to a solid community of support and the walls and gates were restored. This is the premise of restoring lives with the twelve gates. As a small group of wounded people begin the process of restoration together, it is imperative that someone in the group be reliable and trustworthy. The group will learn faithfulness through faithfulness.

## Chapter 6

## Nehemiah Restored More Than Just the Walls of Jerusalem

Nehemiah rebuilt the twelve life gates as well as the city gates for the people of Jerusalem. Nehemiah brought reality to the people of Jerusalem by explaining the need for good walls and gates. He restored authority to them by soliciting their help in the process. He helped them recover their belief in God and the goodness of God as well as the protection and security of God. Nehemiah restored their self-esteem by encouraging them to work and not be afraid. He restored their trust in themselves, in God and in his authority. He empowered the people of Jerusalem by holding them accountable. He restored their freedom with the gates and boundaries, he restored relationships with the people in the city and those who came to help them rebuild. A new harvest was expected because the pillage was stopped. The Israelites had a new sense of belonging and their joy was restored at the completion of the gates and walls. All of these factors are important in the restoration and recovery process.

Nehemiah restores reality by confronting the situation as it existed. In chapter two verses seventeen and eighteen he said, **"You see the trouble we are in: Jerusalem lies in ruins, and its gates have been burned with fire. Come, let us rebuild the wall of Jerusalem, and we will no longer be in disgrace. He also told them about the** gracious hand of my God on me and what the king had said to me."

In verse eighteen of chapter two, Nehemiah heard the answer. The people told him that they would rise up and build. **"So they strengthened their hands for this good work,"** the Bible says at the end of verse eighteen. The reality of any situation often brings a positive response to "get to work" and make the changes needed.

Authority restored comes almost immediately behind the initial start for Nehemiah. At once his authority and the power of God for restoration are challenged by the evil Sanballat and Tobiah. They laughed at the people of Jerusalem and made jokes about their work. But Nehemiah begins to show the people the godly authority on his life by responding to the enemy: **Nehemiah 2:20, "The God of heaven will prosper us; therefore we, his servants will arise and build; but ye have no portion, nor right, nor memorial in Jerusalem."** Throughout the book of Nehemiah, he is challenged but because of his authority as a servant of God, he is able to stand and complete the tasks he is given.

We see the belief system of the Israelites has been restored in chapter eight as Ezra and all the people gather together and read the law. The people lifted their hands in verse six of chapter eight and worshiped the Lord with their faces to the ground. **"Ezra praised the LORD, the great God; and all the people lifted their hands and responded, "Amen! Amen!" Then they bowed down and worshiped the LORD with their faces to the ground."** What a sign of restoration of their belief system that was for the people.

The self-esteem or respect for self is restored by Nehemiah in chapter four as he helps the people overcome the opposition of ridicule and discouragement. Nehemiah prayed to God to turn their reproach on the heads of those who ridiculed the Israelites. When the attack on the self-esteem of the people continued, Nehemiah continued to pray to God for help. As they became discouraged Nehemiah spoke words of encouragement to the people. He restored their self-esteem through prayer and through encouragement.

Trust was restored as day by day the workers saw that Nehemiah would not leave them and that he worked side by side with them. They began to trust him with their lives and as that happened they began to have trust restored in their own lives.

Nehemiah empowered the people through prayer, working with them, helping them accomplish goals and not giving up. Throughout the book of Nehemiah we are told that Nehemiah prayed and talked to the people but more than that he worked with them. In verse twenty three of chapter four he said that **"He nor his brothers not his servants stopped working long enough to wash their clothes."** How much that must have empowered the people to stay with him and complete the work in their lives.

As the walls were completed, their future was restored. No longer would they have to redo the work they had done the day before because intruders had destroyed everything. No longer would these people have to look to the past for hope, because now their families were safe and they could accomplish much.

As the walls were rebuilt and the gates restored neighboring peoples helped the Israelites. In verse five of chapter three it says that the Tekoites repaired the walls. **"The next section was repaired by the men of Tekoa, but their nobles would not put their shoulders to the work under their supervisors."** Tekoa was a town in Judah which was thought to have belonged to the tribe of Asher. The nobles of Tekoa would not help the people of Jerusalem, yet some of the townspeople came and helped in at least two sections of the wall. This is only one way that relationships were restored.

A new harvest was restored when Nehemiah cleansed the defilement out of Jerusalem and asked God to remember him with the first fruits of the new harvest.

Nehemiah restored belonging to the Israelites as we see the provisions for the Levites were restored placing the priesthood in the proper position to set the "church" or the worship back in its rightful place.

Finally, joy was restored to the city as they celebrated the dedication of the wall. In verse twenty seven of chapter twelve the people were told to keep the dedication with gladness, thanksgiving and singing. **"At the dedication of the wall of Jerusalem, the Levites were sought out from where they lived and were brought to Jerusalem to celebrate joyfully the dedication with songs of thanksgiving and with the music of cymbals, harps and lyres."**

The walls were built, the gates restored and the people were joyous because their lives were now restored with hope and a future. Jeremiah told the people that God would restore their future when they were first being taken into captivity. **Jeremiah 29:11,"For I know the thoughts that I think toward you, said the Lord, thoughts of peace and not of evil, to give you an expected end."**

We are looking at four specific areas of restoration. The first area is the restoration in the area of a relationship with God. In the spiritual journey, finding God is part of the first steps in the recovery process.

Second, we will study the need for restoration with self. This includes becoming aware of self from a biblical perspective. As we study the need for restoration with self we are to walk humbly before God. **Micah 6:8, "He has shown you, O mortal, what is good. And what does the LORD require of you? To act justly and to love mercy and to walk humbly with your God."** Also in the recovery of self, addiction or life issues cause what many call "losing self." As we find self, we discover empowerment to move to restoring our complete life.

Third, we will study restoration to others. Finding God, finding ourselves and then being restored to others is a sometimes difficult path to follow, but as we go along rebuilding our boundaries we will discover that this difficult path leads to serenity.

Fourth, we will study the restoration to community. Often reputations are destroyed and the community in which we live is reluctant to accept us. We will study the need to be restored to community in our path to full and complete recovery.

No recovery process is without problems. In our study you will discover that life is worth living regardless of the difficulties we must overcome. The slippery downhill slide of addiction was never the uphill fight that recovery must be. In recovery we are building, in life's hard issues we are tearing down and destroying. Different "muscle groups" are required in recovery. In fact, no positive "muscle groups" are needed to slide downhill. All we need to do is give in to gravity. With recovery we are climbing up, one step at a time, one day at a time. The uphill climb is not without commitment. It is one day at a time with a lifetime commitment.

At the Valley Gate, the East Gate, and the Old Gate our relationship with God will be restored. As we rebuild the boundaries and the gates that hold this relationship with God we will move on to the Inspection Gate, the Fountain Gate, the Horse Gate and the Prison Gate to restore self to self. We will restore the new self, or in the words of Paul in **Colossians 9:10**, **"Do not lie to each other, since you have taken off your old self with its practices and have put on the new self, which is being renewed in knowledge in the image of its Creator."** As we put on the new man we will then begin the restoration to others through rebuilding the Dung Gate, the Fish Gate and the Vendor Gate. Finally, at the Sheep Gate and the Water Gate we will be restored to community.

# Chapter 7

## The Valley Gate

### Restoring a Relationship with God Begins in the Valley

Recovery begins in the valley. It is when we have come to the end of ourselves, when all hope in ourselves is gone and we can come to the point of recognition that we need help. The help that we need is not in what we can do for ourselves, it is in a source outside ourselves. To get to this point we have to go down almost to the depths of despair before we can look to God. God did not plan that we need to go to despair to find Him. He simply meets us there.

Valleys are a common occurrence in the terrain of the land of Canaan. The city of Jerusalem is nestled on four mountains and is situated in the Judean Mountains. The four mountains on which Jerusalem sits formed a kind of moat around the city which protected it by natural means from enemies, especially when the walls and gates were in place. Historians say that when the Babylonians captured Jerusalem it was only because of the internal dissension the army was able to take the city. With this natural protection in place and the protection of God plus the walls and gates of the city, no enemy should ever have been able to penetrate.

But because of deep neglect of God's plan for life, Jerusalem had been laid bare by captors about seventy years before Nehemiah. When the Babylonians captured Jerusalem they took all the best young people, the strongest men and the prettiest women. The people left were what today society calls marginal. Marginal; that is some strange word to use for people. It simply means the poor and simple minded or in other words the vulnerable. Left in a city on a hillside with limited resources and limited skills, seventy years took its toll on the community.

The Babylonians were ruthless conquerors. They burned the city, burned the gates, knocked down the walls and took everything of value. They even buried the water supply outside of the city, covering up the wells and springs. The poor, ravished people were left to hide in caves and roam the country side looking for food. Not much had changed over the seventy years of captivity for the nomads of Jerusalem. When Ezra brought the first group of Israelites back to rebuild the city they found ruins and a great ancient metropolis devastated.

According to the book of Ezra the returning refugees started at once on rebuilding the temple but got distracted by the needs of their own families. They stopped working on the temple and began building their houses and businesses. It did not take long for the natural safety barrier of the valleys below to become highways for pillagers. The refugees struggled to maintain their footing as roaming bandits hit night after night and stole their wares.

The people were tired and discouraged when Nehemiah arrived. They wanted a revival, what they got was reality. The Israelites had a way of thinking that whatever they did God would rescue them even if they did not follow His instructions. They thought they lived in a spiritual bubble. Days of grinding, building, and rebuilding of their homes prepared them for the reality of the situation to hit them square in the face. They needed to get right with God. They needed to ask for help, admit they had a serious problem and choose to forgive. They were caught in the denial of thought which left them redoing their houses because their house was their castle and in that castle they were king. King of the castle was a symbol of control at least that is what they thought.

Nehemiah assessed the situation and then he asked the people to join him in rebuilding the gates. He told them the unadulterated truth. The city was never going to succeed as a city for God until the walls and gates could be rebuilt.

Each section of wall and each gate was rebuilt by a certain group of people. Some of the rebuilders were joined by bands of those marginal people who had struggled to regain some footing in nearby villages. Such were the people of Zanoah who joined with Hanun to rebuild the Valley Gate. It was near Zanoah, a city on the outskirts of Jerusalem, where a great underground water system was found by archeologists. Archeologists say the water system was completely buried, possibly by earlier conquerors of Jerusalem. These people lived in the valley of Hinnon. Hinnon was a desperate place. It was, as we said earlier, where idol worship was practiced by Israel. No doubt the inhabitants of Zanoah participated in the worship of Molech.

Idol worship was characterized by sex, prostitution, and sacrifice. There must have been many bones in the Valley of Hinnon. Bones of the bodies of children, of older people left for dead, of warriors dying in battle over some slice of bread or keg of water. The name Zanoah means forgetfulness or desertion. As with all biblical names the town was known for its forgetfulness and desertion. Perhaps the history of the people in Zanoah was to run away and to forget responsibility, but when they banded together to help Hanun rebuild the Valley Gate they made a decision to change. They must have, by their actions, admitted the problem of irresponsibility and stepped up to help rebuild the city gates.

As we begin our journey to full recovery and restoration we will have to admit the problem and make a step to rebuild our lives. Addiction is riddled with irresponsibility. How many times have we failed to take the responsibility for our actions? We have blamed and complained and used excuses until we have nowhere else to go but to face reality. The inhabitants faced reality. They needed help from Jerusalem. They needed to be able to come inside the gates when an enemy attacked. They needed to make some simple changes.

As the Valley Gate is restored in our lives we accept reality. What is reality for most of us in recovery? One reality is that the problems of life have overcome us. We are no longer able to function normally. Life has become controlled by the problem. I need help.

The very hinges of the gate at the valley could have been forged with the words "I need help." The lock to the gate at the valley could have been the desire to forgive the past mistakes made by the Zanoahians and by those who buried their water supply. The key to the gate could have easily been made of reality dripping with the sweat of real people, with real problems, working towards a real solution.

Our Valley Gate, the place at the lowest point in our lives, will be hinged with "I need help." It will be built with beams made from responsible actions such as seeking a recovery program or joining a recovery group. These responsible actions will help correct irresponsible use of drugs or alcohol or some other negative activity. The first responsible action will be to get a detoxification of the negative behaviors or addiction. The lock to the gate will be the steps to forgiveness taken. Choose to forgive yourself, choose to forgive others. The key will be made of a real person, admitting a real problem and working towards a real solution. The key will always work at this gate. Reality will open and close many gates and hold many boundaries.

A real person needs help. The help must come from outside his norm. As we look at how the Valley Gate was built and the walls which held the gates rebuilt, we notice that someone outside of the group from Jerusalem helped to rebuild. These people were unlikely to help, yet there were many outsiders who helped in the restoration. God is an unlikely source of help to most people. What we know about the Bible or God is most likely from movies or cartoons or felt Sunday school characters. To think that God could help means to surrender. Surrendering to a power greater than ourselves takes courage. Surrendering to a power we know nothing about takes exceptional courage. How can we accept or even ask for help from God when we know so little about Him?

At this gate we must accept that God exists and that He can help us. We call that faith. Some call it desperation. A friend of mine told me that desperation did not appeal to him in finding God. He wanted to find God on equal footing. The only thing about trying to find God on equal footing is what good will that do for a dying man? When we are down, we must look up. We must find strength to reach out to that "higher power" whose name is Jesus.

It is an amazing thing what God does in a situation like ours. Like those people of Zanoah, God sees the need for help. He just shows up on the scene with tools in hand. Now Hanun could have looked at the unlikely help and said "no thanks, I got it." But he realized that the help was needed, no matter what the source. We can do that very thing. God has shown up on the scene of our problem. He has all the necessary tools to help us. It is up to us to accept the help and begin to work with Him. Hanun and inhabitants of the low country rebuilt their wall. What will you do?

One of the valleys that the Bible speaks about is the valley of Elah. In I Samuel 17:2 the giants stood on one side of the valley and the Israelites on the other. This was a valley of decision and a valley of victory.

In the story of the valley of Elah, a giant named Goliath taunted the armies of Israel mocking God and everything that they believed in. Goliath spoke curses to the Israelites and they accepted the curses and cowered under the intimidation. Each day the giant grew bigger in the eyes of the poor soldiers. They became more powerless every time Goliath bellowed his negative accusations. What could they do? The solution was too simple and too ridiculous. Fight back? How could the weak, powerless army fight back?

Fear had gripped the armies of Judah and pride had empowered the giant. The haughty laughter of victory ran through the giant Goliath and the Philistine army. The plan to overcome was simple. Believe in a power greater than yourself. That is what David, the smallest of his family, said.

Believe in a power greater than yourself? That was the question the brothers of David must have been thinking. Well, David didn't use the exact words but the meaning was the same. David, the youngest of his family who carried cheese sandwiches to his brothers in war, had a brilliant plan of action to win victory over Goliath.

He said to Goliath as he ran twirling his slingshot, "You come to me with a spear and a sword, but I come to you in the name of the Lord."

Across the ages I can hear those who have conquered life's hardest problems say to the giant intimidator, "You come to me with chemicals and disease, but I come to you in the name of the Lord." David won the battle over the giant Goliath not by being the bravest soldier, but by looking to God as his outside, most unlikely source of strength.

When a person comes to the point of discovery the problem has overtaken their lives, this is a low point. This is a valley. In the valley emotions are intense. A person is scared and intimidated. Things are bleak on one side of the valley but on the other side is hope because discovery leads to decision. Just as David looked across at the face of the giant and said he would face that giant and take him for the cause of God, so can we look across the valley of decision and see the victory that waits. At the Valley Gate was the Hinnon Valley. In the winter the valley was filled with torrential waters but in the summer the valley was dry.

There are many references to valleys in the Bible which can help us understand the restoration of the Valley Gate. One such is the valley of Achor. The English translation is the Valley of Trouble.

Joshua had led the Israelites into a victorious battle at Jericho. With the strong help of God and His plan the people of Jericho were smitten and the Israelites were on top of the world with thanksgiving and gladness for winning this victory. God gave specific instructions about the loot that was left after the battle. The whole city was burned leaving only the gold, silver, bronze and iron to be taken and given to the treasury of the Lord.

The problem with that was all the silver, all the gold, all the bronze and all the iron was just too much for Achen. After all, didn't a soldier deserve a little something for risking his life? He could not help it if that beautiful Babylonia garment and a few coins somehow fell in front of his eyes. He had to take it. That is what is called coveting. (You can read the biblical account of Achen in Joshua chapters 6, 7,8.) When coveting starts, or sin of any kind, it affects others. Achen's sin cost him and the whole nation. Thirty six men were killed when the Israelites faced a tiny city. Their hearts melted in fear as the citizens of this seemingly easy to defeat town ran at the previously victorious soldiers.

When Joshua sought the Lord for the answer, the Lord told him there was "sin in the camp." When Achen's sin was uncovered, the tribes carried him to the valley of trouble and stoned him and his family to death. This valley of trouble could have been prevented but greed got in the way. If the gate of reality is not restored in the life of the recovering person then the valley that is meant to bring them to God may turn to the valley of trouble and all will be lost. Addiction, as well as other life issues, offers the opportunity to walk through the valley in reality or in trouble. Those sins that cause trouble can be refusing to admit the problem, lying to ones' self, and a multitude of other things that stand in the way of submission.

This is the valley of surrender. It is the valley of recognition and of pain, yet it is also the valley of hope. It is in this valley that we begin our climb to the new life that we desperately desire. It is interesting to note that the rebuilders of the Valley Gate were from the marshland about ten miles away from Jerusalem. Hanun, whose name means graciously given, was a son of Zalaph which means wound. Always in the Bible names were given for distinct meaning. The name would often reflect what the person's life would be or what God's intention was for the family or nation. It would not be hard to see that after a wound God gives graciously to help in restoration.

Such was the Valley of Beracah. Jehoshaphat looked out on the horizon one day and saw a vast army surrounding Jerusalem. His advisors added to his horror by reporting the news to the king that this vast army was from far away and across the sea. Jehoshaphat's life flashed before his eyes and all of a sudden fear grasped his heart. But Jehoshaphat turned to God for help. He prayed and got an answer. The fearful king called for a fast and the whole country began to pray. A prophet came to Jehoshaphat and told him what the Lord said.

Jehoshaphat obeyed the Lord and told his people to trust God. He trusted God so much that he sent his singers out before the army. When the Israelites arrived at the place of battle the enemy was totally confused and had begun to attack themselves. The confusion was so great that the army of Israel did not have to fight at all. It took them three days to collect the spoils from the camp of the enemy. On the fourth day, the king and the people assembled in the valley of Beracah and blessed the Lord. They celebrated the victory over the enemy in the valley. (You can read this story in II Chronicles 20)

The valley can be a place of trouble or it can be a place of praise and celebration. It all depends on admitting the problem, confessing your part in the problem and submitting to God for help.

At the Valley Gate, or gate one, we admit this is the lowest place of our lives and what we need is gracious help. It is a place of facing the reality of our lives, looking again at our lives. We want real deliverance and healing, we want to get out of this situation, this valley. In this valley we must face reality. Nehemiah saw the reality of the situation at the Valley Gate. It was bad, really bad. He needed help. He needed help from God and help from people. He could not tackle this project alone. Looking at the destruction caused him to face reality. This gate, facing the reality that we cannot do this alone, is the first step to change, to reality.

Once we look at the reality, we must make a decision to move to admitting that we need help. It is worse than we thought. We cannot live in denial any longer. In AA they say "I admit my life has become unmanageable." Standing in front of the mirror of reality forces the question "Do I want to be like this the rest of my life?" If the answer is no then there is nowhere to go but up and out. Looking up and outside ourselves we will begin to see a glimpse of the light of God. He will open our eyes to the truths we need for recovery and restoration.

## Chapter 8

## The Gate of Authority

## Restoring a Relationship with God Continues with Recognizing Authority

In the ancient culture of Israel gates were significant to the people for various reasons. The gates were a makeshift court system not too different from our lower courts of today. At the gate property could be exchanged, wills probated, credibility given and politics practiced. Like in the days of King David, Absalom sat at the city gate and heard minor cases for the people. He also wooed the hearts of the people planning a takeover from his own father. It was at the city gates that Ruth's fate was determined. It was there at the gate that Boaz secured the land from Naomi's closest kin so that he might be in position to marry Ruth

Kings and others of importance would often sit at the city gates. In Jerusalem, the East Gate was of most significance. It was at this gate where the High Priest had to stand with the red heifer on Yom Kippur and look through the East Gate into the Holy of Holies. On Palm Sunday, Jesus rode into Jerusalem through the East Gate. This gate symbolized the coming of the Messiah, redemption for all mankind. This gate is the gate of true authority. God's authority to save and change man is symbolized in this gate.

As we look at the gate of authority in our lives we will

find there are at least three levels of authority to be restored. First is the authority of God in our life which must be acknowledged in restoration. Second is the authority that we possess as children of God. This authority is often seen as nonexistent in the life of the broken. Third is the authority of others.

Since God was not created and since He created all things, His authority is from everlasting to everlasting. God's authority rests in His being. He is the ultimate, the beginning and the final authority on everything. He has all power and authority. Yet in his omnipotence, He gives authority to us as believers and disciples. In other words, God's authority is limitless and though He gives authority to us, He still holds ultimate authority. He relinquishes authority to Satan, yet all authority ultimately belongs to God. He operates in pure authority, yet respects the authority that He has given to others.

To recognize the power and authority of God requires accepting personal limitations. Some say we have to resign as master of the universe as we accept and recognize that God is in control and not us. Rebuilding the gate of authority takes submitting to the appropriate authority that God has. Realizing that God is the ultimate authority begins to quash the resistance in ourselves that makes rebellion so attractive. He has the final say or the last word in everything.

Accepting God as the ultimate authority may take some work since for many the authority figures in life are often less than appropriate in their setting good examples. A father or mother may abandon their child or abuse them emotionally setting up negative ideas about authority figures in a child's mind. Teachers, police officers and even pastors may neglect their responsibilities and a child or young adult will assume that all authority figures are untrustworthy.

God made man in His own image, according to Genesis twenty six, giving mankind a natural love for his creator. This natural love for man's creator is a spiritual desire which manifests itself in a physical and emotional way. For example, a young girl is adopted at birth. Given away by the natural mother, the child is placed with a loving and responsible family. But before she knows she is adopted, the child feels there is something missing, a hole in her heart, so to speak. When she learns of her adoption, she wants to know her natural parents. It will not matter too much what kind of parents the natural mother and father would have been. All the girl wants is to know her "creator." Her natural creator was her natural mother and father. This girl may search the world to find her "creators." This natural, emotional desire for parents is part of the DNA that God put in all mankind to know the creator. I know what some of you are saying, "Not everybody wants to find their parents." This may be so, but the hole in their heart is still there to know who created them and why they were born.

This desire to know the creator is so powerful that man will fill the "God hole" with anything that gives temporary relief. The hole will be filled with lovers, drugs, sex, money, power, children, you name it. But the hole must be filled.

When a person turns to drugs or alcohol or sex or gambling the hole for the creator is temporarily filled. Pleasure fills the hole for a season, but it will never fill it completely or effectively forever. As drugs or the substitute for the creator becomes less and less effective, the hole becomes more and more empty. The search begins again. As recovery begins, the search may take a turn towards filling the God hole with other things such as meetings, people, and good deeds. Fear may even take over the search because God may seem austere and very scary. This is simply because God represents ultimate authority and all the authority a person in early recovery may have known was abusive, overreacting or absent.

A leap of faith is needed to find God and to recognize that God's authority is lifesaving, not life ending.

At the East Gate this leap of faith is preceded by examination of the possibility that God can restore a sound mind. Recovery is a restoration of the sound mind. Examination of who God is and what He is capable of will initiate a leap of faith to rebuild the authority in our lives.

The scriptures reveal who God is and what He is capable of in our lives.

**Exodus 34:5-7, "Then the LORD came down in the cloud and stood there with him and proclaimed his name, the LORD. And he passed in front of Moses, proclaiming, "The LORD, the LORD, the compassionate and gracious God, slow to anger, abounding in love and faithfulness, maintaining love to thousands, and forgiving wickedness, rebellion and sin. Yet he does not leave the guilty unpunished; he punishes the children and their children for the sin of the fathers to the third and fourth generation."**

Numbers 23:19, "God is not a man, that he should lie, nor a son of man, that he should change his mind. Does he speak and then not act? Does he promise and not fulfill?"


Deuteronomy 3:24, "O Sovereign LORD, you have begun to show to your servant your greatness and your strong hand. For what god is there in heaven or on earth who can do the deeds and mighty works you do?"

Deuteronomy 4:24, "For the LORD your God is a consuming fire, a jealous God."

Deuteronomy 4:31, "For the LORD your God is a merciful God; he will not abandon or destroy you or forget the covenant with your forefathers, which he confirmed to them by oath."

Deuteronomy 6:4-5, "Hear, O Israel: The LORD our God, the LORD is one. Love the LORD your God with all your heart and with all your soul and with all your strength."

Deuteronomy 9:3, "But be assured today that the LORD your God is the one who goes across ahead of you like a devouring fire. He will destroy them; he will subdue them before you. And you will drive them out and annihilate them quickly, as the LORD has promised you."

Deuteronomy 10:17, "For the LORD your God is God of gods and Lord of lords, the great God, mighty and awesome, who shows no partiality and accepts no bribes."

Deuteronomy 20:1, " When you go to war against your

enemies and see horses and chariots and an army greater than yours, do not be afraid of them, because the LORD your God, who brought you up out of Egypt, will be with you."

Deuteronomy 20:4, "For the LORD your God is the one who goes with you to fight for you against your enemies to give you victory."

Deuteronomy 33:27, "The eternal God is your refuge, and underneath are the everlasting arms. He will drive out your enemy before you, saying, 'Destroy him!'"

Joshua 1:8-9. "Do not let this Book of the Law depart from your mouth; meditate on it day and night, so that you may be careful to do everything written in it. Then you will be prosperous and successful. Have I not commanded you? Be strong and courageous. Do not be terrified; do not be discouraged, for the LORD your God will be with you wherever you go."

Joshua 23:3, "You yourselves have seen everything the LORD your God has done to all these nations for your sake; it was the LORD your God who fought for you."

II Samuel 22:32-34, "For who is God besides the LORD? And who is the Rock except our God? It is God who arms me with strength and makes my way perfect. He makes my feet like the feet of a deer; he enables me to stand on the heights."

Psalms 10:4. "In his pride the wicked does not seek him; in all his thoughts there is no room for God."

Psalms 33:11-13, "But the plans of the LORD stand firm forever, the purposes of his heart through all generations. Blessed is the nation whose God is the

LORD, the people he chose for his inheritance. From heaven the LORD looks down and sees all mankind."

Psalms 37:30-31, "The mouth of the righteous man utters wisdom, and his tongue speaks what is just. The law of his God is in his heart; his feet do not slip."

Psalms 46:1-2, "For the director of music. Of the Sons of Korah. According to alamoth. A song. God is our refuge and strength, an ever-present help in trouble. Therefore we will not fear, though the earth give way and the mountains fall into the heart of the sea."

Psalms 48:14, "For this God is our God for ever and ever; he will be our guide even to the end."

Psalms 54:4, "Surely God is my help; the Lord is the one who sustains me."

Psalms 59:9-10, "O my Strength, I watch for you; you, O God, are my fortress, my loving God. God will go before me and will let me gloat over those who slander me."

Psalms 62:7-8, "My salvation and my honor depend on God ; he is my mighty rock, my refuge. Trust in him at all times, O people; pour out your hearts to him, for God is our refuge. Selah."

All other authority may be questionable, but God's authority is never questionable. The scriptures prove that God is able to restore us to a sound mind and fill the void that is in our lives. All we have to do is accept His authority.

Though we admit we are powerless over our addiction, we must never accept that we are powerless in Christ. Jesus has given us the power or the authority to be the sons and daughters of God.

In Luke, Jesus gave his disciples power and authority to trample on snakes and scorpions to heal the sick and deliver the demon possessed. When we recognized the authority of God in our lives and become children of God, He gives us authority. This is a gift. God empowers us to accomplish feats we never could before we recognized Him. This newfound authority sets us in a position as an overcomer and not as a limp, powerless individual bound by an enemy within. The authority God gives us is to overcome and conquer that enemy of addiction.

The Bible uses two different words for authority which are interchangeable with power. According to Strong's 1847 the word authority used by Jesus to tell His disciples they had authority over the devils and diseases is the Greek word *exousia* which means power of choice or liberty of doing as one pleases.

If we are given authority as the children of God to do as we please we must learn to exercise our authority in all our life choices. Satan knows we have the power of choice and can do as we please, so he begins to persuade us to use our authority in a negative context. Take for example addiction. We have learned that addiction subdues our power to make right choices. But if we go one step further with the biblical definition of authority, addiction deceives us by telling us we have no choice. Let's go one step further in the deception. Satan knows that we have authority, or that we can do what pleases us, so he gives us opportunities to be pleased by negative choices. Think about it this way. Because we can do what pleases us, we choose cocaine. The power of cocaine or the authority of cocaine is like that of a king, it forces submission. We

continue to do as we please making the authority of cocaine stronger until we do not want to do anything else. As Christians in addiction we may feel stuck. The Devil has used our authority against us. This is why we must wait for the addict to want to get better. Without that authority of the person, they will always remain an addict.
'

Authority must be recovered in the life of an addict. To recover authority from the drug or behavior we must want to change. That "want to" can only come with an internal desire from God. It is a special grace for the recovery to begin. That special grace is Jesus. We will always want to do what pleases us because we have been given that authority by Jesus.

The problem is not that we have no authority. The problem is that we do not use the authority God gave us appropriately.

The final restoration of authority at the East Gate is the authority of others. We must restore some authority of others in our lives. Accepting the authority of the law enforcers of our country is a huge step for a person in recovery. Accepting and restoring the authority of others to choose their boundaries is another step for those working on recovery. This may take some doing on the part of the person in recovery because again, some of life's hardest problems are sustained in rebellion.

All of the aspects of authority can and will be restored as a person in recovery practices the personal disciplines of prayer, meditation and submission. Prayers of surrender are included in our workbook for the *Twelve Gates of Recovery and Restoration.*

We have refused authority for so long. The pillars that hold the gate of authority in our lives must be rebuilt. Being teachable is one strong pillar that must be set in place in our lives. An attitude of "I know it all" causes rebellion of authority to creep into the framework of our character. To become teachable we choose to listen. We listen with an attentive ear. Teachable people may know what another is speaking about, but they listen to hear something new. The other important pillar of the East Gate of authority is respect. As we allow authority in our lives again, we choose to respect the office and the person. Respect is given. It is often said that respect is earned, but because of where we have been, no matter what the person has done we must choose to respect their humanity and the office that they hold.

Restoring the gate of authority in our lives has many applications. We must accept the authority and responsibility for our own lives. So much of the responsibility and authority has been relinquished. We have given up the authority over our children and our personal character. Area after area of responsibility is relinquished. We have refused to take authority over the things that we can change. We think we can't speak or act in our own behalf.

At this gate, the East Gate, judges decided the fate of people; they ruled on laws and settled property disputes. Legal problems were handled at the East Gate. As the gate of authority is restored, legal problems begin to get under control. We become less and less afraid of the authority issues in our lives. Our destiny is also reestablished because our destiny is so often determined by how we relate to God's authority and the authority of others.

## Chapter 9

## Old Gate

## Restoring a Relationship with God through Basic Beliefs

The Old Gate of the city of Jerusalem was on the western side of the city. It was thought to be the oldest gate of the city and may have been originally built by the Jebusites who occupied the city before King David made it the Holy City. The city represented the heritage of the peoples of Jerusalem. For hundreds of years people from every tribe came into Jerusalem. There would have been no reason for King David to destroy the gate. He used what was there as part of his defense system for the city.

The Old Gate was also called the Jeshanah Gate. This word Jeshanah means storage. It might be said that this gate was "old storage" for the people rebuilding the city. It had stood the past and rebuilding it would remind them that the past was important as long as it was part of the present and the future, bringing protection to the city and not destruction.

The past is where basic beliefs are formed. Basic beliefs are those beliefs that are central to your makeup. Such beliefs will include what you believe about God, family, community, yourself and others. These central beliefs must be restored because some beliefs are truth and some are lies.

The sons of the original builders of the gates of Jerusalem had a part in rebuilding this gate. They were the sons of Levi, the first group of priests to minister to God. Traditions of the word of God, morality, and humanity were rebuilt here.

Faith in God must be established. Our decisions must be turned over to God's care. We must restore the things of God to our lives. At this gate we must restore truth, and that truth must be based on the word of God which the never changing truth of God.

**Jeremiah 6:16 states, "Thus says the Lord, stand by the ways and see and ask for the ancient paths, where the good way is and walk in it; And you will find rest for your souls."**

We may be feeling a little overwhelmed with the newness of recovery. This reminds me of the story of the children of Israel as they began to walk over the sands of the desert in search of a new home. They were hot, tired and scared of the new enemies they faced. They had little water, they were struggling. The memory of Egypt was so tempting. They forgot the hardness of the life of brick making and building for Pharaoh. All they could remember was the taste of onions and sweet water. They only remembered the times when the families celebrated with feasts. The Israelites wanted the familiar regardless of the cost. They wanted to go back to where they came from. The promise of the new life seemed so far away, when the old familiar life was so close. This may be where you are this week. You may want to go back. Nobody ever told you that the way to freedom was hard.

They only told you that freedom was good. Well, it doesn't seem so good right now, stuck in the limbo of the desert. So, what can we do to continue the journey? We can submit.

"You have got to be kidding", you may be thinking. You may still be in the pre-contemplation stage of thinking about thinking about changing. That sounds redundant, but reread that statement. Thinking about thinking about changing is a very real stage of change. Somebody else has thought about you changing but now you are being forced to think about it.

Begin to imagine that your life is a walled city. This city has definite boundaries and entrance and exit points. The city has a central point and that is the temple. It has structures and buildings and walls. It can maintain itself for a season. This walled city has been ravaged by enemies, wild animals and neglect.

When an issue strikes you, it leaves you defenseless. It leaves you with no boundaries. Your walls and gates need restoration. When Nehemiah toured Jerusalem he looked for what needed to be rebuilt. He was concerned with the destruction, of course, but more than that he was looking for a place to start. He needed a plan.

God gave him that plan as he passed through the Valley Gate and then through the Dung Gate. That plan included a team of workers. The plan included more than he could do alone. He had to have help. He had to ask for help. Nehemiah called the city leaders together along with the other residents. Nehemiah told them that it didn't look good. The gates were completely destroyed. It was going to take a lot of work to get the gates and the walls restored. He needed their help.

The one thing about the gates of Jerusalem that many forget is that all the gates were being rebuilt at the same time. It took fifty plus days to rebuild all the gates. The builders worked side by side and took no breaks until the work was completed. They did whatever it took to get their city protected. It is the same thing that must be done as you work to rebuild your life. You must be willing to work diligently on the restoration plan until recovery is well established.

At this juncture you must make a decision to believe the truth about the past, the present and the future. It is where you decide that the way you have been living is not working and give up control to Jesus. The bible says that Jesus is the way, the truth and the life. At the Old Gate you begin to realize that Jesus can restore truth in your life. He promises the Holy Spirit to you to bring you into all truth. The truth restored in your life will also restore traditions from the past and make traditions for the future.

Being brutally honest will not be easy. What may seem perfectly honest to you will seem like a total lie to another person. Denial is the basis for so much of the dishonesty. There are at least three types of denial. First, there is simple denial in which a person denies the fact of an unpleasant reality altogether. Next is minimization in which a person admits the fact but denies the seriousness of the situation. Finally there is projection in which a person admits that there is a problem but refuses to take responsibility for it.

People also will rationalize behaviors rather than admit the truth about what the behaviors are doing to others and to themselves. The problem may be bad, you may rationalize but it isn't as bad as some other problem you may have encountered. Another defense mechanism people use to keep from being honest is reversal. When being confronted with the issue in your life, you may reverse the conversation by pointing out the problems in the confronter's life.

All of these behaviors are identified as defense mechanisms. But what are you defending? Are you defending your right to be broken? Are you defending your right to continue in negativity? The truth is very hard to face at times.

You will look at the fact that issues affect every part of a person. It is a spiritual, mental and physical problem. Issues do not just affect you but reach into the lives of your loved ones and often takes over their lives as well as yours.

God designed us to be a triune person. Mankind is spirit, soul and body. The human spirit is where God meets man, where man meets God and where man meets others. The soul is the mind, will and emotions of a person. This is where man meets with circumstances. It is where personality lives and where character is built. The body is the flesh and blood of an individual; this includes the organs of the person such as the brain. This is where man meets environment.

**Ephesians 2:1-2**, **"We were dead in our trespasses and sins."** That is, before you came to Jesus. When you came to Jesus your spirit was quickened and now your human spirit is alive to Christ and dead to sin. It is in the human spirit that the Holy Spirit comes to take up residence. It is in the human spirit where discernment resides. In the human spirit prior to being born again the person is able to meet another person and assess if that person will be "good" or "bad." When a person is born again, the Holy Spirit comes to sanctify that human spirit and teach the human spirit the ways of God. Now the human spirit makes connections with others who have the Holy Spirit residing in their human spirit. As the Holy Spirit has more encounters with man, the human spirit begins to "walk in the spirit." The Holy Spirit encounters man through prayer, through Bible reading, through friendships with other Christians and many other ways.

The human spirit begins to be converted or changed thus sending out change signals to the mind, the will and the emotions. What we think has a huge effect on the way we feel and the choices we make. The way we think, act and feel has an enormous effect on the way we meet circumstances in our lives. As the human spirit is converted our personality begins to be converted or changed. The environment where we live thus will be effected as our spirit and soul is converted. This is change from the inside out. Some call this a heart change. This heart change comes to us as we meet God through Jesus Christ. In our heart or spirit we decide God's morality and His traditions and His values help us to restore a broken relationship with Him. Through the belief in Jesus Christ as our savior we are now open to building a trusting and caring relationship with Him through accepting and participating in the traditions of God rather than the traditions of man.

## Chapter 10

## Inspection Gate

## Restoring a Relationship with Self

Shakespeare once said "To thine own self be true." At the Inspection Gate, also known as the Miphkad Gate, a person can begin to restore a relationship with self by honestly taking a look at who he was, who he is and who he wants to be.

The Inspection Gate was known as the Miphkad Gate or the place of the appointment. Temple servants and merchants restored this gate. They were well acquainted with the need for a gate which held merchants accountable. It was at this gate the temple materials were counted during King David's reign. King David was the greatest king of all Israel. During King David's reign he had materials brought to Jerusalem to build the first temple and those materials came into the city through this gate.

As you might expect the people at this gate inspected all the wares, materials and items used in the temple. They were accountants. The temple servants may have helped to repair this gate. Because of its proximity to the temple, it led directly into the temple.

As a spiritual correlation to the natural, this gate inspected or took account of what was coming into Jerusalem. It is at this gate that we inspect ourselves. We must look at all of our life at this gate. We must inspect ourselves. Inspect myself are two words that will take your breath away when you are already having trouble facing yourself. The inspection must be searching and fearless. Searching implies that we will have to look for the things in our lives which we will have to take into account.

Fearless means without fear. It is very scary to look into our lives and write down the things that we have done, said, haven't done and can do but won't. It is very scary to look at ourselves as we have become. However, it is necessary if we are to go forward.

After surrendering to God your mind has cleared from the fog and you are probably sleeping better. Some of the hardest part of detoxification is over, but you may not be ready to face all the reality that positive thinking brings.

In the recovery work of restoring a relationship with God you were looking at something outside yourself to help you get your mind back. That something turned out to be God. He has begun a work that He will continue in you. First you looked up, now you look in. It may be more difficult to look in than it was to look upward.

When I say restoring you to self, I am really meaning the work of forgiving yourself. If you will be honest the first three gates have helped you forgive God for not being who you wanted and expected Him to be. We have always wanted God to be the God of our understanding and when we find out that in order to really help us we need to see Him as the God of the Bible. This may mean that we have to "forgive" Him and then ask Him to forgive us for thinking that we know better than He does.

We have to look at ourselves and forgive ourselves for being the "bad" person and to accept ourselves for the "good" person that we are. This can take some time so be prepared for a few days of inward inspection and a few days of emotional upheaval. It may take more than a week to really look at ourselves. It may take years. Nevertheless, let us begin now to look at what our lives really are. When I say good person I mean the good behaviors, not the ability to be "good" like God. The "bad" person means the bad behaviors that are done.

This is a moral inventory; therefore we make a list of the good morals as well as the bad. Morals are another way to express boundaries. Boundaries are how far we have gone, or how far we won't go. As we make a list of our boundaries we are also taking an inventory of our gifts, talents, abilities, what we have wasted, what we have abused, things we have but have failed to use. As we take this inventory it is good to look at all of our life issues.

No matter how terrible your life has been, there have been some good times. We must make an inventory of the good as well as the bad. We must look at what can be salvaged and what must be thrown away.

Again, this will take some time. So don't get in a hurry for this. If you start with the inventory you will soon discover that the inventory evokes emotions and memories that sometimes have been lulled to sleep by life. The period of time when the emotions are half asleep and half-awake can be very uncomfortable. When your physical leg falls asleep and it begins to awaken, you feel all the nerve endings and almost wish that the leg would remain asleep. But, of course, you know better. You can't walk with your leg asleep, you allow the leg to get fully awake in order to better utilize the leg.

## Chapter 11

## Self

Self, what do we know about it? It is indeed mysterious. "Who am I?" is a question people have asked throughout time. Knowing self is part of the very first sin of Adam. When the serpent tempted Adam and Eve, the temptation hinted of being someone else other than who they were. "You can be like God," the serpent promised. This timeless question is centered in accepting so much about God, about others and ultimately about what your role in life is.

Discovering who you are will take inspection. It is inspection of your failures as well as inspection of accomplishments. Inspection of where you have been and inspection of where you are going are all a part of finding self. You will explore the design of God for your life and build boundaries to protect self that will allow you to grow to be the person you want to be. The boundaries that you have allowed in your life have not accomplished very many good things. At this junction of restoration you will tear down and build up. You will tear down those walls that have kept you bound to negativity and build up the walls and gates for a positive and healthy life style.

Miphkad in the Hebrew language means numbering, mandate and an appointed place. Today you will begin numbering or naming your achievements and your failures.

This is a mandate or command for you if you wish to move forward in recovery. Then, at the appointed place which in the word of God implies a specific place for a specific purpose, you will offer these achievements and failures to not only be recognized but to be surrendered.

Remember when the walls and gates of Jerusalem were being rebuilt everyone was working on all the walls and gates at one time. This simply means for you that the first three gates of reality, authority, and beliefs are now added to the inspection of your life.

It is so important to continue to stay in reality as you inspect your life. As you say "I need help" looking to God because God can help, you can say "I can believe" the truth about myself in my past and in the future. Without the help of God, you will not be able to look at where you have been and where you are going. As your relationship with God builds from reality to authority to a new belief system, you can say "I can look at myself with forgiveness, having received the forgiveness of God." There will be no need to look at self until you have admitted that you need help, committed your life to God saying "God can help" and submitted by saying "I can believe." Without God you will see your achievements with pride and refuse to look at your failures. Or, you will look at your failures and be stuck there forever. It is here you begin to face you. It is here that the hard work of restoring self to self begins.

As the gates of Jerusalem were being rebuilt there was much unrest by the enemies of the city. Nehemiah faced continual assault from Sanballet and Tobiah. The assault was so oppressive the people were told to hold a weapon in one hand and work laying bricks with the other. Nehemiah refused to come down off the wall.

Determine for yourself that you will not stop rebuilding your life until it is secure. Many people will not understand your determination. Some will even try to stop you, but you must continue the inspection and continue to rebuild each area of your life until you have a new life.

## Chapter 12

## Fountain Gate

## Restoring Self through Building Trust

The Fountain Gate most likely led to the Pool of Siloam. It was very important for the ancient people to have safe water inside the walled cities. For Jerusalem, the best water was known to be at the well of Jacob just outside the city gates. When an enemy attacked the city, the enemy would often cut off the water supply holding the city hostage. This gate would be extremely important for the people to restore since it protected the fresh water supply for the people.

Restoring the self is equally important. Restoration of a relationship with God will certainly lead to the restoration of self, since God is our creator and He knows best what our purpose for life should be. It stands to reason as we acknowledge God we will begin to acknowledge our "self." As with the restoration of the walls and gates of Jerusalem, the restoration of a relationship with God flows into a relationship with self. Then the restoration of self to others and self to community continues. Looking at the city wall reconstruction we can see a spiritual correlation to recovery. **I Corinthians 15:46, "First in the natural then in the spiritual."**

It is thought that the Pool of Siloam was fed by an aqueduct built during the reign of King Hezekiah. The Gihon Spring north of Jerusalem was the source of the water in the aqueduct and the Pool of Siloam was the overflow pool for the water. All fountains must have a source. The Gihon Spring was the major water source for the area around Jerusalem and was one of the reasons Jerusalem could survive. Without drinking water a culture could not exist. The spring was channeled down to the city by a great manmade aqueduct.

Ancient civilizations learned the technique of forcing water through small pipes or passageways causing pressure and forcing the water up and out of a fountain head. Such was the case with the fountains of Jerusalem.

Jesus healed a blind man by telling him to wash in the pool of Siloam. The fountain was a symbol of fresh water, flowing water. Fountains help to add air to the water and keep the waters moving providing fresh clean water for drinking and cooking and cleansing. This pool at the Fountain Gate was the major supply of water to the city.

Jesus referred to a fountain of living water. As a person confesses to God and to another human being, the corrupt and vile things that he has done flow out and the new fresh water of life flows into him. There is such a refreshing when true confession is made. As self is restored there must be a flowing of the old out and the new flowing in. An emotional healing takes place as that flow begins.

So many people have said to me they do not know

who they are. They must find themselves. They must be restored to themselves. It is as if negative life events have robbed them of their soul. The physical body is there, but the emotional part, or what we call the soul, is gone. That part of the soul is defined in modern terms as the mind, will and emotions: the personality.

Trust must be rebuilt. To rebuild trust will require vulnerability. That vulnerability takes place when we share the truth about what we have been, what we are now and what we want to become with another human being and God.

When the stale, stagnant water is expelled from the pool by the fountain and the fresh water flows into the pool the waters are kept fresh and safe for others to drink. This is a metaphor of what the healing of the emotions will be like. Through confession of all the dirty secrets, raw emotions flow out and allow the fresh clean healing of joy to fill hearts creating new positive emotions and healing.

It is interesting that the Fountain Gate is located near the Kidron Valley. Traditionally the Kidron Valley was a place of destruction for the idols that Israel so often worshipped. When a new godly king would take over Israel he would often have the idols torn down and burned in the Valley of Kidron. This a yet another picture of what can happen as the negative emotions are changed to positive emotions through the cleansing of confession.

How can trust be restored and emotions healed and negative driving emotions changed to positive emotions? Healing comes through three phases. These phases are interwoven in the mind, the heart and the soul.

Emotional healing comes first as a definite decision to choose to be vulnerable. Vulnerability means to be willing to be hurt again. You may have decided long ago that you would never let yourself be hurt "that way" again. But the truth is that you have continued to be hurt over and over again in the same way. Once you made that decision, you were locked into a prison cell of angry emotions. Choose to be vulnerable.

The second phase of healing comes when you decide to get involved with people again. By this I mean really interacting with people. Simple, shallow relationships are not enough to find healing. Interacting with people on a deeper level may open wounds that have scabbed over but not healed underneath. The initial reaction can be painful, but once the wound is exposed the healing starts.

The third phase of healing is opening your heart to love again. Love is a two way street. Love must be received as well as given. You have to receive love where you find it. Love is all around. You must recognize it and receive it. Love is in the cashier at the grocery store, the children you see, the old people at the nursing home, the people at work. The song that says "If you can't love the one you want, love the one you're with" says volumes if you think about it. Stop wanting the ones who have hurt you to love you and start accepting the love from the ones you are with.

# Recovery of Addiction Explained

# Part 2

## Chapter 13

## Addiction Recovery Explained

The story of redemption is also a story about addiction recovery. Jesus was sent to earth on a mission from His father to recover what had been lost in the Garden of Eden. Sin entered the world and began an avalanche of destruction which has driven mankind deeper and deeper into sin which he cannot get out of by himself. The first story of recovery told in the Bible could be the story of Lot and Abraham. Lot was kidnapped by sinful kings and Abraham went after him to recover his belongings and his life. Abraham was on a mission of recovery and restoration. Likewise, Moses was sent to recover and restore the Israelites to God, to themselves, to others and to a community. The Israelites needed to be restored to God, to who they were originally intended to be, to each other and finally restored to a thriving community.

The pattern of recovery from the effects of sin whether it is drugs, alcohol, pornography, depression, or life threatening illness is found in the Bible. The pattern for recovery and restoration is simple to learn but complicated to follow. In this book you will discover how the pattern works. We will follow the deliverance in Exodus and study the restoration of the gates of Jerusalem in Nehemiah.

## Biblical Meaning of Recovery

As we begin our journey to addiction recovery let's start with the Biblical meaning of the word recovery.

According to Strong's Concordance 5337 the Hebrew word for recovery is *natsal*. This word which is translated "recover means to snatch away, deliver, rescue, save, strip or plunder." This word recover is used in I Samuel 30:8 when David prayed and asked God if he should pursue a group of renegades who had stolen his wives and looted his camp. The Lord answered him by telling David to pursue the renegades and to recover all that had been stolen from him. When a loved one has been ravaged by addiction or other hard life circumstance recovery is necessary. Sometimes the recovery process will be as though being rescued from an enemy that has plundered the best you have. Those caught in addiction have been plundered of the gifts that God has placed in them from birth. They need to be rescued and restored.

Another Hebrew word for recovery is *Chayah*, according to Strong's Concordance 2421. This means to live, to have life, remain alive, sustain life, live prosperously, live forever, be quickened, be alive or be restored to life or health. When a person is recovering from addiction or another of life's issues he or she will need to be given a sustainable life. Jesus intends for us to recover from life's issues by having a sustaining life and prospering life.

Ahaziah, according to I1Kings 1:2, fell down in his chambers and was sick. **"Now Ahaziah had fallen through the lattice of his upper room in Samaria and injured himself. So he sent messengers, saying to them, 'Go and consult Baal-*Zebub*, the god of Ekron, to see if I will recover from this injury.'"** He sought or enquired from a source other than Jehovah as to whether he would recover from his disease. This is exactly what is happening to the myriad of people who are "sick". They are seeking recovery from sources other than from the one that can give them full recovery.

A balance of godly wisdom is what we need. We must begin to recognize the power of God and to use all the tools and resources available for recovery from addiction and various other life issues.

Of course, when God has provided medications for recovery those medicines should be used. Where God has given knowledge about the body, the emotions, and the spirit we should utilize those tools. God has given much knowledge and wisdom for the natural as well as the spiritual.

*Michyah* means to restrain, halt, stop or to retain. *Shuwb* means to turn back to God or repent; to turn back from evil. The word repent is often defined as changing the mind. A working definition of recovery from the biblical sense is stopping negative behavior by changing the mind to accept positive attitudes and actions.

In the New Testament, Paul tells Timothy that they may "recover themselves out of the snare of the devil who are taken captive by him at his will."

<u>The Message</u> in **II Timothy 2:26** says it this way, **"Run away from infantile indulgence. Run after mature righteousness—faith, love, peace—joining those who are in honest and serious prayer before God. Refuse to get involved in inane discussions; they always end up in fights. God's servant must not be argumentative, but a gentle listener and a teacher who keeps cool, working firmly but patiently with those who refuse to obey.** *You never know how or when God might sober them up with a change of heart and a turning to the truth, enabling them to escape the Devil's trap, where they are caught and held captive, forced to run his errands."* (italics mine)

This last sentence explains in a nutshell what happens when a person gets out of addiction. Addiction is a trap. People are caught and held captive and forced to do things that are evil. As we study the addiction process you will see exactly how people are manipulated into the deception of addiction.

## Who Needs Recovery?

Who needs recovery? In some form or another everybody needs recovery. Everybody has lost something, whether it is material loss, or the loss of a loved one. Everybody has at one time or another had to stop doing something. Everybody has been sick or known somebody who was sick. Everybody needs recovery.

How does recovery happen? It happens through restoration to God, restoration to self, restoration to others, and restoration to community.

## Restoration to God

The first area of restoration is that of self to God. Restoration to God has three specific parts including admission, commission, and submission. Admit your need for God, commit your failures to God, and submit your life to God.

Human beings have built into their DNA a desire to direct their own lives. They are taught from a young age to be self-sufficient. Babies are nurtured to be independent. Toddlers learn "me" before any other word, except mama. They learn to call mama first because somehow they know that she will help them with their "me." Even those of us who are brought up in the church still have a hard time understanding that we need God. Many think we will need God at death or in a crisis but never on a day to day, moment to moment basis. When the pain of life shows up, and only after we have tried everything else first, we might turn to God for help. This is why we might hear someone say "they haven't hit bottom yet." It is believed that when one hits bottom one has nowhere else to go but up. It doesn't matter how one gets to the understanding that he or she needs God, it only matters that he or she gets there. Without understanding one needs help, and that help must come from God, recovery will never begin. A person may stop drinking or doing some other destructive behavior for a while but without God, relapse is inevitable.

When a person admits the need for God, then he or she can come to the revelation that all their failures must be committed to God. The failures of life are sometimes the most cherished things a person possesses. That statement may seem unusual, but failures cushion addiction. The failures of life can form a bed for excuses. A person who wants to stay in addiction will find that using their failures as an excuse leads to blaming someone else. If it's someone else's fault then it will be another's responsibility. The addict is then relieved of personal responsibility and their failures form a comfortable place to stay addicted.

If a person commits their failures to God, then God can take their failures and use them as a foundation for learning and change. Committing failures to God holds a person accountable for past mistakes and requires him to learn from those mistakes. Some studies have indicated that failing to learn from past mistakes is a "disorder" that happens to all addicts.

Finally, in being restored to God, a person must submit his or her life to Him. This submission may also come in stages. Since God is a triune God; Father, Son and Holy Spirit, the submission has to be to the total personage of God. God must be submitted to as the father that He really is. Because many people have not been exposed to godly fathers, the thought of submitting to God as father may be extremely difficult. A person needs to learn that God is a loving authority, a faithful provider and completely dependable. If they have no experience with an earthly father who loves, is faithful and dependable, the person may resist submitting his life to God the father.

Submitting to God as Jesus the son may also cause some difficulties. Jesus is savior, redeemer and lord and must be seen as all three for a person to submit his or her life completely. Since many have been betrayed by a man, this can cause some issues in surrender.

Finally, submitting to God as the Holy Spirit may seem spooky to some. Many people have a misconception of the Holy Spirit. They may not believe in the Holy Spirit at all, so submitting to God as the Holy Spirit to be their friend, counselor and helper may take some time. Surrender to the Holy Spirit comes through an intimate knowledge of God.

Surrender and submission includes repentance. **II Peter 3:9, "The Lord is not slack concerning his promise, as some men count slackness; but is longsuffering to usward, not willing that any should perish, but that all should come to repentance."**

**Acts 3:19, "Repent ye therefore, and be converted, that your sins may be blotted out, when the times of refreshing shall come from the presence of the Lord."**

**Acts 8:22, "Repent therefore of this thy wickedness, and pray God, if perhaps the thought of thine heart may be forgiven thee."**

**Proverbs 28:13, "He that covereth his sins shall not prosper: but whoso confesseth and forsaketh them shall have mercy."**

When you come to God you repent by changing your mind about Him.

## Restoration to Self

The second stage of recovery comes with restoration to one's self. In addiction of any kind a person loses self. The self that must be restored is the one God intended a person to be from birth. No person was intended for addiction. No one's life ambition is to become addicted and out of control.

What does it look like to be restored to one's self? I relate it like this: a person must be able to trust himself again. Even in the worst addict I have ever known there are still some boundaries that are set and that the person will not cross. For example, one addict won't steal from family but will steal from strangers. One addict will not harm an older person, while another will not harm a child. However in most areas of the addict's life there are no boundaries. In order to trust one's self again the addict must restore the boundaries of his or her life. These boundaries can be restored through forgiveness. First one must receive forgiveness from God. In recognizing that God is the ultimate good and that one has no way of making it right with God, one must then humble himself to take the gift of forgiveness through Jesus Christ from God. Forgiveness is never earned. It is a gift from God. The word is for/give/ness. Right in the middle is the word "given". It is freely given and must be completely received. Forgiveness empowers a person to change. It softens hard hearts and changes minds.

After a person receives God's forgiveness, then he or she must give forgiveness to himself. You should understand that what has happened in the past is not going to change. Forgiveness does not change the past.

Forgiveness changes your view of the past. You cannot go back to yesterday and redo it. You can begin today to let go of the past failures. Commit the past to God and give yourself a gift of forgiveness.

Finally in restoring self to self, a person must make restitution to one's self. The only way to make this restitution to one's self is to change the behaviors which caused the problems. This step cannot be left out. You must be able to trust yourself and you will not be able to trust yourself if you continue to do the same sinful, addictive behaviors. Self-forgiveness restores the soul.

**Psalms 23:3"He restoreth my soul: He leadeth me in the paths of righteousness for His name's sake."**

## Restoration to Others

Specialists say the first stage of recovery usually lasts one month for every year in addiction. They also say that a person stops maturing emotionally on the first day the first drink is taken. If you begin at the first day of the first drink or the first cigarette, the addict can take years to be restored to full recovery. Take into consideration that the years spent in addiction were most likely in a premature state and an addict can do a lot of damage to relationships.

Pre-mature refers to the stage the brain is in before complete maturity. It is speculated that the cognitive brain is not fully developed or mature until age twenty four, meaning that any drugs or alcohol or addictive behavior done before that age stunts the maturity of the individual. This pre-mature state means that an adult who is forty acts like a thirteen year old. Imagine the havoc a thirteen year child could wreak in a forty year old body.

Relationships to parents, to children, to a spouse, to co-workers, and friends can all be in complete chaos in the life of a person who has serious addiction issues.

A person may be right with God, may even have trust in one's self, but to restore self to others can take years. In restoring one's self to others the process of confession, honesty, repentance and complete forgiveness has to take place. An addict also must come to terms with personal responsibility for restoration to others to be effective.

In restoring self to others, the pre-mature has to grow up. A grownup understands the damage that has been done to some or all relationships. Damage to the relationships must be repaired with work from both parties. A person has no control over whether the relationship will be restored to a previous state, but he or she does have control over how he or she will behave towards that relationship.

The recovering person will at first make an effort to forgive the other person. They must then seek forgiveness for what they have done to the other person. This may come in the form of an apology either in person, by phone or written. But, no matter how the apology is given, sincerity is the key. Humility and sincerity will go a long way to restore a broken relationship. Humility and sincerity may not always bring a restored relationship, however. The recovering person must be willing to give the injured party time to heal.

Making restitution is yet another way to restore relationships. The injured party will have little excuse not to forgive the injuring party if he or she is making every effort to "pay back the offense." One of the best ways to make restitution is to keep promises through faithfulness and commitment.

Restoration must be made first to the family, then to friends and finally to acquaintances. This restoration must reach to the co-worker, the neighbor, and the stranger.

The King James Version of the Bible uses the word family one hundred twenty three times in seventy six verses. God believes in family and relationships. He wants families restored and relationships healthy.

**Ephesians 1:5, "His unchanging plan has always been to adopt us into his own family by bringing us to**

himself through Jesus Christ. And this gave him great pleasure." (NLT)

Luke 8:39, "'No, go back to your family and tell them all the wonderful things God has done for you.' So he went all through the city telling about the great thing Jesus had done for him."

**Psalms 38:11** sums up the way an addict ends up. **"My loved ones and friends stay away, fearing my disease. Even my own family stands at a distance."** Loved ones and friends stay away from them, fearing what the addiction will do to them. The family and those closest to the addict will eventually stand at a distance.

## Restoration to Community

The community is affected by the way the addict has lived. People love to think that nobody knows "covered up" life of addiction. They convince themselves that nobody talks about them because they are anonymous. The truth is that most communities know the troubles of the addicted. The community knows about the person with the "problem." People may not know exactly what is wrong but they know something is wrong. The work place is affected, the church family is infected and the neighborhood is involved.

The community restoration begins with a steady job for the person in addiction. This job requires steady and faithful service for restoration. The job must be honorable. There can be no absenteeism, no employee theft, and no bad mouthing the job.

The restoration continues in the community when the one who has been addicted begins to volunteer in the church or in the community. The addict can rebuild his or her reputation in the community by giving back to the community.

Serving the church is yet another way to be restored to community. In the community of church the person is to be held accountable and can safely mature emotionally and spiritually.

## Chapter 14

## When We Ignore Recovery

"Sundays are rough around my house," he said to me. "What do you mean by that?" I asked. "Well, if she is going to have an episode, it's going to be on Sunday morning." Tears were dripping from eyes that were weary of looking for a solution to a major problem in his life and his wife's life.

The man sitting across from me was a well-known retired minister. He was well acquainted with Jesus and the word of God. Sitting next to him was his wife of many years who was well acquainted with drugs.

The weary family took turns expressing the pain of what had happened to their loved one. She, however, sat quietly with a far off look in her eye. In the middle of the serious discussion about how to help this "first lady" she urinated on the sofa.

Her husband told of time after time on Sunday morning when she would lock herself in the bathroom and begin screaming obscenities at him. Pill bottles left empty by her bed or on the floor were the tell-tale sign of a major devastating addiction.

The minister admitted that he had known about the problem for years, but "in his position" in the church as head of a major Pentecostal denomination, he was ashamed that he could not get her "delivered."

It all started about twenty years prior when a nurse in his church offered his wife a Valium. His wife was under a lot of stress trying to meet the needs of the women in the church and to maintain the perfect appearance of an up and rising minister's wife. The Valium was a "lifesaver." At first he himself encouraged her to use the drug, because it made her seem more at ease with the congregation. The nurse kept her supplied and for a season all was well.

What the family did not know is that Valium is a highly addictive drug. Once a person is hooked on Valium the chemistry in the brain begins to change. The natural God given chemicals stop producing and when the person doesn't get the drug of choice or the chemicals it has become familiar with, withdrawal symptoms begin.

As a result of the "unknown factor" this Christian pastor's wife began to experience some withdrawal signs. It is important to know that when you take another person's prescription, especially a scheduled drug (by scheduled drug I mean one that the government tracks as addictive) you have broken the law. I am sure the nurse schooled the pastor's wife on this information. When she began experiencing "symptoms" of what felt like a nervous breakdown, she told her doctor the symptoms, leaving out the important part of the story which was the Valium addiction.

With all addiction, the process is progressive. One pill at night at first is enough. It makes you sleepy and does the job to calm the nervous system. That is why they are called central nervous system drugs. But the tolerance level grows, withdrawal symptoms continue and a person must have relief.

Just a sidebar here, to tell you that central nervous system drugs work in the brain since that is where the central nervous system begins. In the middle of the brain it is speculated that most of the God activity occurs. If that is true, the central nervous system drug does its magic in the brain and the person using the drug loses all spiritual feeling. In a sense they are "dead" to the things of God because their feelings are so numbed.

This pastor's wife had what I call a "little help from her friends." She continued to take Valium, then added pain pills, then added any pill available. This is the quick progression of drugs in your system.

She did not go to the streets to buy drugs, she went to her doctor. As the addiction progressed and her mind was more and more numbed, her feelings completely changed and the love she once had for God was destroyed and replaced with the idol of central nervous system drugs.

On the day she arrived, she was not really interested in change. The family was interested, but she was only interested in being numb. The drugs had changed her thinking; her rational brain was so affected that she could not begin to understand the consequences of her behavior. By this point she would take any kind of pill she could get her hands on. On this particular day she had gotten some over the counter medicines for allergies and taken so many that her bodily functions were out of her control.

The secret and the shame is what landed her in a mental institution for life. She "dried out" going through hallucinations, evil visions, and radical homosexual behavior plus scaring the socks off the rest of the women in our ministry. The once beautiful pastor's wife who led hundreds of women was reduced to a "servant of Satan" in her own words.

Once the drugs were gone, the woman began to crave the feelings of being on more drugs. That insane behavior drove her from our ministry into the streets where her family rescued her. This was extremely difficult because they did not want to rescue her, but what do you do? They sent her again to another treatment facility, but she ran away from there. Keep in mind that this woman was in her sixties.

She was given a sound word of advice that if she did not fight to get free from the drugs she would end up in an institution with bars for the rest of her life.

What a sad story! This story haunts me as I continue to work with addicts. Here's what I have ascertained about addiction from this woman.

First, secrets kill us. Pride stops us from asking for help. The church has a façade of perfection. When a less than perfect person finds her way into the church, rather than marring the façade, she keeps her secrets. The secret of course is not only hers, but her family's secret as well. Her husband can't expose the issue because what will they think in the ministerial association?

Second, the church has failed with people who need recovery. In the case of this pastor's wife she had been taught all her life that her sin was forgiven. In an altered brain where rational thoughts are destroyed, that one truth becomes perverted. This addict believed that no matter what she did Jesus will forgive her and instead of understanding the power of forgiveness to change, she used it as an avenue to continue to sin. Paul addresses this attitude, but with an addict whose brain is altered there is no explaining that grace is not a license to continue in sin.

Third, we need help. The church needs help to understand the surmounting issues of addiction. Sometimes, I believe that Christianity has reduced itself to a form of paganism by using drugs to expand the mind and "go deeper in the spiritual world." This is a personal opinion. I say this because so many in ministry smoke or drink a little. As you will learn later, cigarettes are called the "perfect drug." They hit on every major brain receptor and alter the flow of chemicals in the brain. If you are nervous, smoke. If you are hungry, smoke; if you need to relax or need a "pick up" smoke. Alcohol is a system depressant but one drink begins the chemical change in the brain. This is one reason alcohol helps people who drink to unwind, drink to be social, and drink to go to sleep. The chemicals alter the brain immediately. There is also the matter of the millions of pain pills, which are narcotics, which are given to church folks every day. So, if you think about it, is there anybody who has not altered their brain? Of course then there's caffeine and don't forget sugar and carbohydrates.

America is an altered society. The church is an altered church. As for addicts, well, let's just say that some of us are still living with secrets. Here's the real problem, the church has become a hiding place for addicts to continue using or a place of ignorance about drug treatment. Jesus said the truth will set us free. The church needs to know the truth about addiction and then addicts will be set free.

By the way, the minister's wife did not become free from her addiction. The last time I heard from her she was not doing well. There is a point of no return for some. Not everybody gets free of addiction. This is the ugly truth.

# Chapter 15

## Sin-Disease Concept Explored

On any given Sunday morning people come to church looking for answers. People who have been taught to have a faith in God will often go to church looking for ways to make God relevant to what is happening in their lives. People going through divorce, through financial failure, those going through depression or anxiety all show up a few times at church. Convinced that God has the answer, they try the church all too often to find that the church members do not know how to help. Since to so many God equals a church or church member God then becomes a non-entity who, if He exists at all, doesn't care about what is going on in their lives.

When people can't find the help they need in the church they don't give up, they search for something that looks like what God wanted the church to look like and then they settle to try to find at least a little bit of the help that they need. One such place is Alcoholics Anonymous. A.A. has become the secular church, a place of hope and healing for addicts and alcoholics. The program has been so effective that they have anonymous organizations of all styles based on the original twelve step program. All the church does is beat the organization to death by saying "we don't need another twelve step program."

Christians must be willing to look at the Bible and find its own method of recovery.

## Sin-Disease Concept

Let's begin this discussion with a new idea called the sin disease concept. Let's look at definitions of both sin and disease and then give you a definition of the sin-disease concept built on the word of God and the current knowledge of addiction.

In both the Old and New Testaments the word sin is used many times. Sin has several definitions whether it is a transgression of the law, an iniquity of the heart or simply a mistake. God refers to sin as anything that does not agree with His word. The Bible talks about a sin nature which we inherited from Adam. Although every person dealing with addiction or one of life's issues has the sin nature, addiction is more than that.

In reference to sin-disease we will define sin as missing the mark. According to Strong's Concordance *Chata* is the Hebrew word for missing the mark. In the Greek, the New Testament uses *hamartia* as missing the mark.

This missing the mark is a picture of an arrow aimed at a bulls-eye. Everybody knows that the bulls-eye is the perfect target, but anything less than the bulls-eye is missing the mark.

Addiction was never in the original plan for mankind. God's perfect bulls- eye for man did not include addiction of any kind. Even if your parents were addicts and their parents were addicts and you believe it is in your DNA to be an addict, this is not God's plan for your life. When a person begins to use drugs or alcohol or to begin any behavior that changes the brain chemistry, they are aiming their life at a bulls-eye but missing the mark that God has designed for their life.

Stealing, lying, and adultery are all sins done in deed. Works of the flesh are listed in the Bible as sin. Sin is not always purposeful and intentional. Some sin is unintentional. *Every* man, woman, and child is born with a sin nature which is inherited from Adam. Adam and Eve first sinned in the Garden of Eden and the Bible is clear that sin entered mankind from that day forward. Everybody, no matter who they are, needs a savior because of the sin nature. Sin that is done in deed can take up residence in the flesh or soul realm of a person. Sometimes psychologists call this personality. I prefer to call it the works of the flesh. According to Paul's writings the works of the flesh must be put to death. He said this about the flesh, "I die daily."

Sin that gets rooted in the flesh of a man or woman can't be cast out. Those sins seem to become a part of who the person is and they must be sacrificed or put to death on the cross of Jesus Christ.

For years the church has taken the stand that addiction is sin, so stop doing it. The church and most of its members say to the addicted "Get over it." That statement makes sense to the sober person, but not to the addict. For most of those caught in some habitual negative behavior, they have tried to get over it. Many have tried to be delivered through a prayer ritual, only to return to worse behaviors.

What is missing in this sin definition? While the church sees addiction as sin, others see addiction as a disease.

## Addiction is Both Sin and Disease

Sin in this case is any action or behavior that violates a standard or code of ethics. For Christians that code of ethics is the Bible. Even if we do not know what the Bible says, the behaviors of addiction easily violate our own code of ethics. We find ourselves involved in activities that we never thought we would be involved in. We have, at the very least, sinned against ourselves by our own actions.

A simple definition of disease is simply dis or not at ease. Addiction has altered our bodies. It has caused medical and mental disorders that are now clinical. We must admit that addiction has at the very least altered rational thinking and caused some chemical dysfunction in the brain. Some of these dysfunctions will not go away. Some of them will be reversed. We will learn more about the functions of the brain in a later chapter.

In the sin-disease concept we learn that we are responsible for our actions that led to the disease but once the disease is in place we have to learn what our responsibility is to keep the disease in remission. This is very similar to any other chronic and critical disease. Addiction is both chronic in that it is not going away and critical in that it is deadly.

The sin-disease concept of addiction is not a new concept. It has been around for several years and more and more Christian addiction counselors are presenting this concept as a viable treatment option. We believe that this concept is the only viable option.

Addiction misses the mark of life in every way. The addiction itself is sin but the activities of addiction are also sin. What addict has not lied, stolen from, manipulated or mistreated another human being? The actions of addiction are also sin. Sin in this case is transgressing the law of God and basic morals of humanity. The disease portion of the sin-disease concept poses the belief that addiction causes physical disease. The disease caused in the brain is the one we will focus on during this study. The brain is changed as the addiction becomes rooted. The chemicals in the brain are changed for life and the only way the brain can recover is to reroute the receptor pathways. This takes time and work. The damage done in the receptor pathways is why most people can't just quit without help. The disease concept also reaches into the emotional and spiritual aspect of the person. Addiction touches all the areas of the individual.

Addiction causes a lack of ease or trouble. Nevertheless, there is always trouble when there is an addiction.

Pathological behavior is habitual, maladaptive and compulsive. Negative addictive behavior is habitual, maladaptive and compulsive. So from those definitions let's get a definition of sin-disease that the church may live with.

Sin-disease is missing the mark of a productive plan for life by participating in behavior that is habitual, maladaptive and compulsive causing much trouble in the life of the person and those around him. What starts out as a slight veering off course of a productive life ends up as a progressive development of negative behavior seeking, vulnerability to relapse to that behavior and a slowed ability to respond to positive rewarding activities.

With any disease there are stages. This is so with addiction. In stage one the results can be very positive with just the normal church activities. The person in early stage one of addiction is usually seeking relief of some pain or is looking for acceptance. In this stage the person can readily change the form of relief he or she is getting. Church activities on Sunday morning and small groups such as Sunday school can make a person feel accepted thus eliminating the pain of rejection. Even physical pain can be relieved at this level with love and support from a church group meeting once a week.

In stage two of addiction it becomes a little more difficult to interact with the normal activities of church life as we know it. The social user may feel uncomfortable discussing his use with those in the church, because of the idea of sin related to addiction. Also, church activities do not lend themselves to the partying social aspect of this stage of use. In other words, most churches don't serve alcohol, drugs or display porn at their meetings. So, for the social user, church activities will be a little dull.

Stage three users will avoid the church like the plague. This is when relationships are being destroyed by the user's behaviors. Many will not be able to handle the ill personality of the user. At this stage the personality is changed and anger is manifested more frequently. The attitude that "everybody is out to get me" will be pervasive and they will be less and less sober.

At stage four, the user is under the influence of the behavior even if they aren't using at this very moment. That is hard for the nonuser to understand. The church will probably be too hopeful about the addict because they are attending church but won't recognize that the actions are still being influenced by the chemicals or negative behavior.

In the typical one to two hour meeting there will be little time for intervention. In fact, if an addict begins to manifest unusual behavior, typically they will be ushered out of the meeting so that others will not be interrupted. In some of our Pentecostal services the addict may even be encouraged to participate in a deliverance service. When the "demon" of addiction will not submit to the deliverance the church becomes confused and even annoyed with the actions of the addict and "sends him on down the road."

If the addict has mental illness, some may be completely lost as to how to handle the day to day actions of the individual. There was nothing in my training to be a pastor that told me how to know when a person is on drugs or alcohol or how to tell if someone is addicted to gambling or pornography. At the same time in all the churches that I am affiliated with there are hundreds of individuals still engaging in these negative behaviors. Mental illness was never addressed in my pastoral training.

## There must be Relief

Virtually all drugs which cause addiction increase the dopamine release in the brain in addition to what specific effects are caused by particular drugs. For example in cocaine use, the brain is stimulated and gets excited but at the same time the dopamine which makes us feel rewarded and happy is increased. The brain is flooded with a release of dopamine which eventually turns off the natural pumps that cause users to feel happy and satisfied. At this stage of addiction, only chemically induced dopamine will cause an addict to feel "good." This is the reason so many are miserable when not using drugs. The simple pleasures do not cause the natural dopamine release because the brain has stopped making it naturally. This one chemical change is enough to make relapse inevitable. Misery must be relieved. Since holding a baby won't release the natural dopamine, the mother of a precious baby will leave the child to find her drug of choice to feel normal again. The feelings of happiness which occur for most when attending church do not occur for an addict. Only the chemical release of dopamine can cause those feelings. You may see an addict in early stage recovery leave church seeking a more "exciting" event.

What does the Bible say about all of this?

**Proverbs 23:29-35, "Who has woe? Who has sorrow? Who has strife? Who has complaining? Who has wounds without cause? Who has redness of eyes? Those who tarry long over wine; those who go to try mixed wine. Do not look at wine when it is red, when it sparkles in the cup and goes down smoothly. In the**

end it bites like a serpent and stings like an adder. Your eyes will see strange things, and your heart utter perverse things. You will be like one who lies down in the midst of the sea, like one who lies on the top of a mast. 'They struck me,' you will say, 'but I was not hurt; they beat me, but I did not feel it. When shall I awake? I must have another drink.'"

## Biblical Perspective on Drugs

In the Bible there is a reference to witchcraft in the Greek language that helps us understand the evil of drugs. The word *pharmekia* is translated witchcraft or sorceries. *Pharmeki*a is the root of our English word pharmacy or drug. It is an easy leap from the meaning of drugs in relation to evil. All witches were to be killed according to the Old Testament. Witchcraft or *pharmekia* was to be destroyed. Drugs influence the mind and can open a person up to dark and destructive forces.

Every person is born with an Adamic nature. This is the nature which passed through DNA from the first man Adam. It is the ability to sin against God without reason. Even the smallest baby has the Adamic nature. Children don't need classes to learn rebellion or selfishness; they already are programmed with this information. This nature cannot be cast out as if was a demon because this nature is part of our being, that is the human being. Because of the fall in the Garden of Eden, mankind is cursed with this nature. It is only by and through faith in the death and resurrection of Jesus Christ that this Adamic nature can be truly dealt with. When Jesus Christ was born in the flesh He took on the war that wages between the Spirit of God and man. As man, He became the Second Adam. The First Adam sinned and broke fellowship with God, the Second Adam (Jesus) restored fellowship with God.

Jesus as man was tempted yet He did not sin. He was tried and He succeeded. Jesus suffered and yet did not give in to the suffering. He was all that the first Adam was supposed to be. Because He was sinless He is the perfect sacrifice for the sin nature. He died to take away our sin, especially our sin nature. Of course this is hard to understand because though we receive the new nature through and by Jesus, we are left to experience the old nature's death which comes by behavioral changes. If we do not choose to change our behavior, we have no experiential understanding of the power of Jesus Christ to change our sinful nature. Our spirit is in right relationship with God through Jesus Christ and our actions come into line with His will as we choose different behaviors. This is the experiential side of the spiritual application.

As the behavior changes are put into practice we can know the power of Jesus to help us succeed with the changes. We have a part to do in the change and He has a part to do in the change. His part is to change our want to and our part is to learn new and better habits. Very simply put, He changes the inside, we change the outside. We change where and how we do things. He changes the way we feel about things.

## The Bible on the Disease Part

The Bible says we are fearfully and wonderfully made indicating that God's design of man is awesome and mysterious. God has allowed science to peek into His design to learn about some of the specifics of how the brain works.

For example, alcohol increases dopamine plus hits on receptors that are normally inhibited in the brain. Alcohol produces dopamine to send a message that whatever is happening to the body is pleasurable. All addictive drugs including alcohol increase the production of dopamine or they make their own dopamine. We need dopamine to experience pleasure so naturally the more dopamine the more pleasure. As you can tell by the brief explanation the consumption of alcohol causes feelings of excitement, changes the mood, causes a person to misunderstand rational communication and interrupts sleep patterns.

When the dopamine levels begin to drop, the neurotransmitters are in a way fumbling around in the brain to try to get the same feeling. This causes the cravings for the drug because the natural amount of the dopamine will not produce the same feeling of pleasure. Over time the brain forms a new pathway around the normal pathway. The natural pathway is damaged by the overproduction of dopamine. When a person stops using drugs or alcohol the brain's reward center has been changed. Therefore depression, agitation, anger and other negative emotions are hard to handle because there may be no natural dopamine to signal the reward center that the person is experiencing pleasure. It takes time, exercise, the proper diet and sometimes psychotropic medications to restore the natural reward pathway. This can take up to five years of sobriety.

When we tell an addict to just quit, get a job, and get on with their life we are in effect asking a person with cancer to ignore all the symptoms or discontinue treatment. Another way to look at the disease of addiction is to think of it like diabetes. Diabetes, when left untreated, can take a person's life. Ignoring diabetes is deadly. Denial is also deadly. Once you have diabetes you must do anything and everything to keep the disease from progressing too quickly. Being in control of diabetes means eating the right foods, getting the right exercise, and taking the medication prescribed by a doctor. Having the disease of addiction in control has a similar meaning. You must continue to do the next right thing in order to be sober. Working your program may be the only way you can keep the addiction in remission.

Addiction affects every part of a person. It is a spiritual, mental and physical problem. Man is a triune person, meaning he is made up of three distinct parts. Man is flesh and blood, which is called the body. Man is a spirit, which means he is a spiritual being. The human spirit is redeemed and becomes filled with the Holy Spirit when it is submitted to God. The third part of man is the soul which is the mind, will and emotions. Man meets God in the human spirit. He meets circumstances through his personality or soul and with his body he meets the environment.

Addictions are not limited to the emotional part of mankind in that they change the way a person feels, what he thinks and what he chooses. Addiction is not limited to the spiritual aspects of man in that it separates the addict from God and from others. Addiction is sometimes called a curse or spiritual problem.

With the sin-disease concept, an addict can be treated as a spiritual being, a physical being and an emotional being all in one treatment. It is with this in mind that we attempt to offer some solutions to addiction.

Treating the physical brain disease can begin by taking a one a day vitamin which helps the chemicals in the brain find the needed nutrients for rebuilding.

Exercise, especially walking for forty five minutes each day, helps the brain to rebuild pathways and change the chemical structure of the brain to a new normal. A balanced diet rich in protein and low in fat and moderate in carbohydrates also helps the physical body be restored. Adequate sleep also restores the brain.

Treating the soul requires work in the area of changing the mind. The mind must be changed from a negative mindset to a positive mindset for recovery to last. When the mind changes, you can hope choices improve. With improved choices or decisions, the emotions eventually come in line with the truth of recovery. Meditation, studying the word of God and memorizing scripture or other positive declarations speeds the healing of the soul from the effects of addiction.

Recovery in the spiritual aspect of the person wounded by addiction calls for prayer, counseling, church or meeting attendance, fellowship with like-minded people, and accountability.

As the addict begins to get sober and stays sober the spirit, soul and body become more at peace. It takes work in all areas to have a sober life. This is also a balanced life. Since obsession is such a large part of addiction, it is important to work in a balanced way in all three areas. Being obsessed in one area could drive a person back to the drug of choice for relief.

Changes come to the addicted person through persistence and determination not to be distracted by anything. It is a lifestyle change. Everything must be reevaluated in light of staying sober.

Even church events have to be evaluated. So many church members are casual drinkers. The addict must be careful not to be pulled into "one drink won't hurt you" by anybody. Jobs have to be evaluated in light of staying sober. If a bar has the only job available, don't take it. If the addict is not an alcoholic, remember alcohol is a gateway drug. One drink for a pill taker or cocaine user could open the door for using the drug of choice.

## Chapter 17
## Dealing with "The Miseries"

"The miseries" is a term I use with women in recovery that sums up all the negative feelings about change. It is a period of time dedicated to seeing and feeling and making everything around you miserable. Nothing looks right, feels right, tastes right, you can't do anything right and nobody else can either during the miseries. This period of time usually occurs when change is imminent. This miseries condition may also exist in other women than those in recovery. I really haven't studied all women, just a few hundred or so who have lived with me trying to find recovery from addiction. This time is really not detoxification, because the chemicals have usually been out of the system for at least a week or two. This time is not prior to relapse, because for the most part the miseries come before there is any time of abstinence. The miseries are just miserable to the person and to those around that person. The thing about "the miseries" is relief from the condition is a must. A person in this condition must get relief. A person just can't go on indifferently with the miseries. This condition won't go on too long because that person will seek relief from past habits if the change doesn't come quickly from a positive direction.

The miseries" become the unknown variable; the variable of real change. Can or will a person move from the miseries into change or revert back to old patterns because change is too hard for them? Dr. Gerald May in his book <u>Addiction and Grace</u> refers to what I call "the miseries" as a desert place. He describes this desert as a place between what was in the past and what will be in the future. Some have referred to what I call the miseries as the dark place, or the dark night of the soul. But no matter what you call it, this place is uncomfortable.

Change is what recovery is all about. Change is hard. Thousands have studied change and many have developed elaborate theories of how change occurs, but my theory is simple: change happens because of pain or pleasure. Change that happens in pleasure is fast and furious. It is like that of taking drugs. A teenager doing well in school, socially adept and maturing nicely, suddenly makes a change for the worse. He starts dressing differently, hanging around a different crowd, and his grades drop. This is a sudden change brought on by the pleasure of taking drugs. Smoking pot, drinking alcohol, or doing speed all produce a euphoric experience which requires more and more to feel the same pleasure. But the pleasure is so intense that a person loves the feeling so much that he is willing to risk anything to have that feeling again. Change brought on by pleasure is fast.

The other way a person changes, in my opinion, is pain. When something hurts a person enough, the long agonizing path to life changes begins. One reason pain change is so agonizingly long is that pleasure aspect. For example, drugs cause the same teenager grief with his parents, maybe even with the police. The pain is there, that is for sure, but after a few days the pain subsides and the thought of pleasure returns. If the teenager has a chance to do the drugs again and he feels the pleasure from doing the drug, he forgets the pain. Pleasure trumps pain over and over again until pain is so significant that the person works on the change. That is, until the miseries set in. It is at this time that change can continue or change can be deflected to a later time. How a person deals with the miseries will determine if real change takes place.

Why do the miseries come? Negative thoughts over past events can cause a person to sink into "the miseries." **Romans 12:2** tells us **"do not conform any longer to the pattern of this world, but be transformed by the renewing of your mind."** What a person thinks is very important in recovery. A person in recovery has to make an inventory of past events, confess sin and replace those events with rich and positive things. Sometimes in this process he or she will dwell too long on the mistakes and the negativity of the past. This will cause a person to go into a miserable place mentally. At this point, he or she should seek help to change his or her mind. If no help comes from a positive source the person will return to the old normal lifestyle. No matter how negative the lifestyle it is his or her normal life. Normal in this usage is considered to mean routine.

True guilt is guilt over something a person has actually done. True guilt is a positive emotion to a person in recovery if he or she will confess that guilt to God and receive godly sorrow which leads to forgiveness. That godly sorrow acts as a deterrent to committing the act again. However, if a person refuses to receive forgiveness the guilt can lead a person to the miseries.

Time is another cause of "the miseries." A person trying to make a forever change in his or her life runs into the time factor. It takes a long time to change and for an addict the words long time do not fit his or her vocabulary. Everything is instant gratification in the world of addiction, so when things take time the addict begins to suffer. This particular type of suffering must be explained and accepted or pleasure will come quickly in the form of a relapse.

People get miserable thinking about the future. They cannot see the future or even begin to picture the future as being a contented place to be based on what their past has looked like. Pressure from family and friends to "hurry up and change" is another source of frustration that leads to misery.

Almost anything can cause "the miseries" in early recovery, but early recovery is not the only place for "miseries." Anybody can get miserable. Miserable is a place during the process of change. But, in order to change, one has to face "the miseries" and allow them to have their way without turning back to the old normal.
The Bible says it like this in **James 1:4**, **"Let patience have her perfect work."**

How does one get out of the miseries successfully? You wait.
**Isaiah 40:31 "They that wait upon the Lord shall renew their strength; they shall mount up with wings as eagles; they shall run, and not be weary; they shall walk and not faint."**

## Chapter 18

## The Brain on Drugs

This is a personal testimony of how I learned that drugs affect the brain. My sister had a stroke. It was a mild stroke which happened one afternoon at her work. She began acting strangely and I was called to see if I could tell what was happening to her. She was very agitated and very confrontational. Her personality was changed. She had a terrible headache. She calmed down when I began talking to her and trying to convince her that she needed help. She refused. I was convinced that something was going on with her physically, but could not convince her to go to the doctor.

She evidently began to "feel better," but her personality and even the way she walked was different. She ran into doorways, she talked out of her head, she had significant mood swings. After a few days of this, she finally was diagnosed as having a stroke in the midbrain area.

What I noticed in my sister looked very similar to what women experience as they began to get sober. Norma Jean, my sister, had to relearn some vital and important activities. She had to, as I learned later, reroute her brain around the injury. In prayer, I asked the Lord to show me if this was what happened to women in addiction.

Science tells us the brain is a complex organ. It controls every part of the body from breathing to kidney function to the feeling in your little toe. The brain is the brains of the nervous system, which includes the central nervous system and the peripheral nervous system. The central nervous system includes the brain and the spinal cord. The neuron is the basic communication unit of the nervous system. Neurons receive information from cells in the body, thus communicating to the brain what is actually going on all over the body. Neurons are what help us to react to external changes. Dendrites are like little fingers that receive information from the body and axons carry information from the neuron.

Neurons multiply at a rate 250,000 neurons a minute during early pregnancy.

There are about 13,500,000 neurons in the human spinal cord.

There are 1,000 to 10,000 synapses for a "typical" neuron.

The cell bodies of neurons vary in diameter from four microns (granule cell) to one hundred microns (motor neuron in cord).

Gray matter- The brains gray matter is made up of neurons which gather and transmit signals.

Neurons- Your brain consists of about 100 billion neurons.

Synapses-There are anywhere from 1,000 to 10,000 synapses for each neuron. There are no pain receptors in the brain, so the brain can feel no pain.

Speed- Information can be processed as slowly as 0.5 meters per second or as fast as 120 meters per second (about 268 miles/hour).

Dopamine is a natural chemical in the brain that controls emotion, movement, motivation and pleasurable feelings. Almost all drugs aim for the brains reward system by releasing dopamine into its circuit.

Let's talk about my sister's stroke again. She learned that her brain had become damaged by the stroke. She also learned that throughout her recovery she would have to retrain her brain to work correctly. Her circuit pathways had been interrupted by the stroke and now she would have to teach her brain to tell her body what to do and her brain how to think correctly by building a new pathway.

My sister found this out through her own stroke. She also found out more details as she helped her son recover from a massive brain bleed. When a person uses drugs, the normal pathway of the reward center is supercharged with dopamine. It is interesting that this dopamine is what causes a person to feel good. The brain is a quick learner. After just a few supercharged runs around the reward center with a drug boost, the brain forms a path of least resistance. The brain not only likes the new chemical boost, but it demands it to make the run around the reward center pathway.

At one of the "curves" in the reward circuit is the brain stem. The brain stem is the place in the brain where all the involuntary activity of the body begins. The brain stem controls breathing and things like that. As the strong chemical boost continues the brain not only demands the boost and enjoys the boosts but also moves the memory into the involuntary brain stem. When this happens the drug of choice becomes the drug of no choice and the person doesn't seem to be able to feel or act normal without the drug.

Just like a stroke victim, the addict must learn a new way of life. The addict must teach his or her brain a new pathway around the reward circuit. The addict must take the drug out of the body for a period long enough to reroute the brain away from the brain stem and back to the natural flow of the reward center. In the meantime, while recovery is going on there are about a million other things going on in the brain. A brain that has been saturated with drugs or alcohol or behaviors that increase the dopamine or deplete the dopamine will take much longer "sober" to create the pathways of recovery.

How will this new rerouting of the brain be accomplished? It will be accomplished on purpose with dedication. The stroke victim must learn to reroute the brain to carry on normal activities such as walking, talking, and remembering. An addict must make a conscious decision on purpose daily to help the brains circuitry be rerouted. Relapse returns the brain to the old route and thus the process must start all over again. The longer the drug use the more entrenched the pathway becomes, or the deeper the rut. The brain can develop new pathways but it takes time and determined work on purpose. In other words, old habits die hard.

Did you know that the body has a bonding hormone? This hormone is what enables mothers to bond with babies and couples to bond together in a relationship. It is the feeling you get when you first meet somebody and know immediately they are "good people."

This hormone is suspected to be the same hormone that causes us to love ourselves, love others and love God. Isn't it just like God to hardwire us to be able to fulfill His commands to us? The Bible teaches us that we are to love God with all our souls and strength and to love our neighbor as ourselves. This is just another example of science catching up with the word of God.

In recent studies, scientists have discovered that we have a personal intrinsic pheromone (PIP) which is depleted in twelve months or less by abuse of drugs and alcohol. This PIP is the first to go in addiction and the last to be restored. There are other studies that indicate that trauma also causes a reduction in this personal intrinsic pheromone.

Because we are triune beings with body, soul and spirit this study helps us to understand the complexities of addiction and why we have not been able to pinpoint the exact cause and cure of this disease. People who have depleted their PIP are antisocial and anti-God and do not care enough about themselves to want to change. The physical aspect has affected the personality and the spiritual components of the person. It may take as many as seven years for the person to have the PIP restored. Can you see why we have so many church problems? People are so altered by the misuse and abuse of their bodies that they cannot possibly have good relationships.

Americans like chemicals so much that about fifty per cent of us could be considered abusers of such chemicals. That is a staggering number.

If fifty percent of the people sitting in church pews are chemically altered, what does that say about our church relationships? I will venture to guess. This could mean that what we call worship is nothing more than a chemical reaction. This could mean that church business is being decided under the influence and not the influence of the Holy Spirit. I believe drug use is so common in America that it should be expected and not a surprise to ministers of the church. The lack of PIP in our members and church goers could be why it is so hard for people to commit to one fellowship or long term relationships of the "religious sort." Chemical brain changes due to drug use and abuse is almost the norm in our churches today. Without the help of the strong discipleship programs in our churches to address the use and abuse of drugs and alcohol, we cannot expect our churches to be healthy.

Psalms 139 says we are fearfully and wonderfully made. We are also told that our bodies are the temple of the Holy Spirit. It is time that we recognize the importance of mind, body and spirit in the healing process. We must learn how to take care of our soul, our body, and our spirit to be forever changed.

Exercise, meditation and prayer plus small accountability groups based on the positive and powerful word of God are three ways to restore the PIP that is lost in drug use.

A lady was doing some work on the streets when she met this very sick woman. The woman was dirty, smelly and physically and emotionally worn. I felt sorry for her as soon as I saw her, but didn't really know how much she wanted help. I didn't know it at the time, but the woman hadn't eaten for several days and hadn't slept in at least that many. She had not had a bath in a month. She had been living on the streets in our town prostituting for drugs. She was a seasoned cocaine user. Her dealer had sold her body for payment, but she was so unkempt that her boyfriends didn't want her. Now she was at my house.

The lady left her with me as the woman agreed to stay. She wanted help, at least a shower and some food. I helped her get some clean clothes, offered her a towel and some soap and made her some dinner. She was quiet that day and for several days to come. She was studying and thinking about what she would say to me. One day I learned her story. She had children who were with other family members. She wanted them back. She had sobered up enough to begin feeling guilty for leaving her children.

This is common among women who had abandoned their children for drugs. I explained to her that I could not or would not help her until I knew she had one year of sobriety. The one year would help her stabilize and give her and the children a chance to make a new start. But she couldn't wait. She had AIDS and was in need of treatment. I begged her to get treatment. The drugs had made a rut in her brain that her pattern was to find a way to get money and then get out of treatment, get her kids back to get more money, and to continue her drug use and prostitution.

When a woman wants money and drugs along with a lifestyle that goes with the drug use nothing will keep her from going. This woman was in a safe place, a place to get medical help, financial aid and could have gotten her children back. I could not say by medical evidence like a PET scan that her brain was forever altered, but by her actions there was no doubt. When the trigger came, which by the way was money, she was on her way backward. Back to the streets, the drugs and to the fatal lifestyle of indiscriminate sex.

I wish I could tell you she stopped doing drugs. I wish I could tell you she was doing good with her AIDS under control, but I can't. There was a house fire in which the young woman lost her life.

There is yet another aspect to the physical effects of drugs. I have known many who have stopped using.

These women have changed their whole lives. No more relapses. They have become powerful active women but then one day they have gotten bad news. The physical aspects of drug and alcohol addiction have caught them. They thought they were long past the time when drugs could have a lasting effect. Then the doctor pronounces the diagnosis of chronic obstructive pulmonary disease or COPD, chronic irritable bowel, pancreatitis or even HIV. Addiction causes permanent damage to the body in so many cases. Addiction causes permanent brain damage to so many. The damage is done, but as we have prayed together not one of these sober women would choose to go back to their old life because they are having physical problems now. No matter what the long term physical effects may be sobriety with the help of Jesus is much better than the early death they would have experienced if they had continued to use their drug of choice.

## Chapter 19

## Emotional Aspects of Addiction

The sin-disease of addiction does not stop in the physical body. The sin-disease permeates every part of the human being.

The question is how does this addiction take over the rational thinking of an individual? Let's explore how sin works first.

**Genesis 3:1-11, "Now the serpent was more crafty than any of the wild animals the Lord God had made. He said to the woman, "Did God really say, 'You must not eat from any tree in the garden'?" The woman said to the serpent, "We may eat fruit from the trees in the garden, but God did say, 'You must not eat fruit from the tree that is in the middle of the garden, and you must not touch it, or you will die.'" "You will not certainly die," the serpent said to the woman. "For God knows that when you eat of it your eyes will be opened, and you will be like God, knowing good and evil." When the woman saw that the fruit of the tree was good for food and pleasing to the eye, and also desirable for gaining wisdom, she took some and ate it. She also gave some to her husband, who was with her, and he ate it. Then the eyes of both of them were opened, and they realized they were naked; so they sewed fig leaves together and made coverings for themselves. Then the man and his wife heard the sound of the Lord God as he was walking in the garden in the cool of the day, and they hid from the Lord God**

**among the trees of the garden. But the Lord God called to the man, "Where are you?" He answered, "I heard you in the garden, and I was afraid because I was naked; so I hid." And he said, "Who told you that you were naked? Have you eaten from the tree that I commanded you not to eat from?"**

From the very beginning of man, God placed inside him the ability to make choices. We see that Adam was given choices about naming the animals and God agreed with the choices Adam made. God placed boundaries on Adam and Eve in the garden. In the original free will choices God limited those choices by placing a "can't do" among all the "can do's". Adam could name the animals, but not kill them. Adam could eat of all the trees, except one. Adam could have dominion over the animals but he could not be satisfied with their companionship. God placed boundaries in the garden. It seems as though Adam and Eve were satisfied with the boundaries at first. They agreed with God and He agreed with them. They were allowed to move freely among the boundaries concluding that God's boundaries were good. We do not know how long this went on, but just suppose it was long enough for Adam and Eve to become settled and complacent. In being settled and complacent perhaps they had never been questioned before Satan came along.

On the fateful day that Eve was tempted by Satan she was questioned. The negative choices were available and of course the best choice was available to her as well. What Satan offered was something that she had never once questioned. That option could be to have something God told her not to have. We all know what happened next.

She took the fruit, ate it and gave it to Adam. With drugs it is very similar. Boundaries are set to prevent usage of drugs but on that fateful day you eat of them and then your eyes are wide open.

When Adam and Eve ate of the fruit, their eyes were opened. Their eyes saw things differently. It wasn't as though God had hidden the fact that they were naked. It was just that now they saw things differently. This occurs with drugs as well. It is not that life is not the same, it is just that the perspective of life is changed. The doorway to seeing things differently is wide open when a person takes the first drug into his or her system. It is wide open if the brain recognizes something that makes them see things differently. The reality of life has not changed at all, but with addiction, the perception of everything is changed.

And these perceptions are insidious. The three perceptions that are most often changed which affect the emotional make up of a person are how a person sees mercy which relates to anger, how a person sees fear which relates to anxiety and how a person sees joy which relates to depression. (This is relative to emotional feelings and is not addressed at this point in the chemical make-up of a person. We will discuss that in the physical changes of the body in addiction.)

## Anger

How a person handles anger is one of the four key components to emotional change as a person gets deeper and deeper in addiction. Of course certain addictive drugs do affect the chemicals in the body which increase the anger component of the emotional stability of a person. It is easy to see this if you watch intervention television programs or police programs showing how addicts are arrested. Some become very violent and extremely aggressive during times of arrest. Even more than that the addict will become extremely aggressive in what would seem to the sober as a simple misunderstanding. Going deeper into the emotional aspect of people, we can see that some addicts who are attempting to get sober are still extremely aggressive and somewhat violent due to what society calls anger issues.

**James 1:19-20, "This you know, my beloved brethren. But let everyone be quick to hear, slow to speak [and] slow to anger for the anger of man does not achieve the righteousness of God."**

There are at least four ways a person handles his or her anger. One way is to suppress his angry feelings. A person who suppresses anger hesitates to express his feelings. He or she will quickly say "I'm not angry" but then plot to avenge the issue. Another way a person handles anger is to be openly aggressive. There is no doubt about this type of anger. It is loud and defined by specific actions, such as slamming doors or loud bodily gestures. Passive aggression is yet another way to deal with anger. The passive aggressive person admits his anger but his need for control outweighs his being exposed by being openly aggressive. The passive aggressive person is one of the most dangerous people. He will often seek revenge from behind the scenes. One other way people handle anger is to be assertive. The assertive person attempts to save his personal self-worth and needs while still thinking about the needs of others.

Suppressing anger, aggressive anger and passive anger all have negative consequences. These ways of handling angry feelings show the least amount of mercy. When drugs are used for a long time a person often loses sight of mercy for others. Let me explain. A person might think that addicts have the most mercy since they have been in desperate situations and have felt the devastation of addiction. You might surmise that addicts will give the most mercy to others in similar situations. But, time after time, when asked if another addict should be shown mercy to return to a program, or given another chance, the addict will say no, they are getting what they deserve. Mercy has been destroyed by the lifestyle of addiction. When mercy is destroyed in a person, anger manifests.

**Habbakuk 3:2, "Lord, I have heard the report about Thee and I fear. O Lord, revive Thy work in the midst of the years, In the midst of the years make it known; In wrath remember mercy."**

It was in God's mercy for us that His anger or wrath was contained. Because God is a God of mercy and grace, His anger does not last forever. God has reasonable issues for anger and thus man can feel the feelings of anger but not lose his temper. Anger is the feeling, temper results in the actions resulting from the feeling.

Preserving self-worth, preserving basic needs and preserving personal convictions are all issues that will stir the emotion of anger. One example I use to explain preserving self-worth is when a person calls another a name the first feeling they have is anger. A person who is called a derogatory name will often get angry immediately. The closer the relationship of the person is to him or her, the more the anger. Some attacks on how a person feels about one's self are much more subtle. Being told how stupid a person is from a young age can set the stage for needing to defend one's self even if that person thinks he or she is being referred to as "stupid." Feeling self-worth is a God given belief. God loves us and gives us value not because of what we are or who we are, but because He says we are valuable. God has planted in our DNA the knowing that we are valuable, regardless of how much we are put down in life.

Basic needs are also implied by the word of God. God tells us that He will supply our needs. He calls Himself Jehovah Jireh, the God who provides. From God we know that our basic needs are important and qualify for protection. When our basic needs such as a place to live, clothing, food, love, nurture, etc. are withheld for any reason, a person gets angry. If a person has had no security in life and his or her needs have not been met, then a person feels angry.

Finally, personal convictions or basic beliefs can be a place in a person's life where anger can easily arise. Personal convictions include what one thinks about life and how life should be lived. It could be how a person feels about the treatment of others. For example, I will get mad immediately if I see or hear about a disabled person being treated with disrespect. My basic belief is that all people should be treated with dignity and respect, so don't treat someone who has a disability disrespectfully just because they can't or won't be able to defend themselves.

Angry feelings are just that, angry feelings. It does seem that people in addiction have a lot of trouble handling anger. When I started Bethesda I heard the Lord say that every woman coming would have two core issues: anger and rejection. So far He has been right.

## Anxiety

Fear is a God given emotion which helps us keep boundaries and protect ourselves and others. Job said in chapter twenty eight that the fear of God is the being of wisdom and shunning evil gives us understanding. Healthy fear is beneficial. The fear that stops a person from picking up a poisonous snake saves his life. The fear that keeps a person from taking drugs or stealing from somebody is healthy and helps to create healthy boundaries.

All of us have fear. Healthy fear is often destroyed by using drugs and replaced by anxiety, or unhealthy fear. A person on drugs has no fear of taking too much of the drug. That same person will enter dangerous neighborhoods to purchase drugs or make dangerous and fearless decisions which could result in death. Unprotected sex with strangers is one action that many who use drugs take without a dread or a fear. Over and over again examples can be given that prove that healthy fear is destroyed through drug addiction. Unhealthy fear is born in drug addiction. Paranoia and anxiety are multiplied in the life of an addict. For years after abstaining from a drug of choice those in recovery suffer from anxiety and one level or another of paranoia.

Anxiety can be described as an unknown fear, a feeling of impending doom. Unhealthy fear can devastate a person for life. This emotion of unhealthy fear is very hard to heal or treat. Paranoia will sometimes manifest in the life of a former addict as thinking that everybody is against him or her. It could show up by someone thinking that everybody is looking at him or her.

Anxiety can manifest in the life of a former addict in medical issues such as hypochondria. The former addict can have anxiety over death, over being sick, over talking to people, or getting a job. Anxiety can show up in almost any area. This is extremely unhealthy and can cause more relationship issues and health issues. Anxiety can create relationship issues. Many healthy people cannot relate to anxiety and often make the matters worse by dismissing the anxiety as something a person can just stop feeling. The Bible says be anxious for nothing. Learning to trust God is the only real cure for anxiety. Relaxation techniques are good to learn and meditation works well for some.

## Depression

Signs of depression are evident in most addicts, both in the using stages of addiction or in the recovery stages. Signs of depression include moodiness, irritability, increased negative thinking, negative perception of events, decreased motivation, negative emotions, appetite and sleep problems, sexual response changes, and social isolation. Withdrawal from drugs or behaviors will usually begin the cycle of depression.

Depression issues are increased due to the chemical changes that occur in the brain and the depletion of those necessary chemicals that stabilize moods. Depression is not always due to drug use or addiction problems but when these occur in a person's life, depression is almost always evident. As with all the emotional issues caused by addiction, depression is greatly relieved by obeying the word of God as it relates to changing the mind and thinking on good things.

**Philippians 4:8, "Finally brethren whatever is honorable, whatever is right, whatever is pure, whatever is lovely, whatever is of good repute, if there is any excellence and if there is anything worthy of praise, let your mind dwell on these things."**

As a person suffers depression, the mind takes a negative turn and will stay in negativity unless challenged. **Proverbs 23:7 tells us "For as he thinketh in his heart, so is he: Eat and drink, saith he to thee; but his heart is not with thee."**

When in depression a person's heart or soul is "not with thee." Their countenance gives them away. As a person in recovery begins to learn the word of God and challenge himself or herself with scripture, negative thoughts begin to be changed to positive thoughts. The more positive a person thinks the less depression a person suffers from. (Of course, we understand clinical depression is a medical condition and must be treated by a physician.) A simple form of depression may be treated with low doses of medication and changing the way a person thinks.

I have personally dealt with clinical depression in my life. What I have found to be most effective is a treatment I have developed for me which considers the mind, the spirit and the body. In seasons of extreme stress I will consult my doctor for a medical treatment which has included Lexapro or St. John's Wort. These medical treatments usually last about six months, which for me is enough time to increase necessary brain chemicals which are often depleted in extreme stress. Medicines are only one way I take care of my body. I routinely exercise by walking or riding my bicycle for at least forty five minutes five days a week. I limit sugary carbohydrates which can spike my blood sugar and then drop my mood in about twenty to thirty minutes. I have spent much effort in learning how my body works in order to keep depression from overtaking me. A psychiatrist who was also a neurosurgeon once told me the best thing I could do for depression was to walk forty five minutes a day. He said that just walking a regular pace for forty five minutes would change the brain chemistry, thus lifting your mood, and changing how you think. I have done this for years and it works!

The second treatment I use to fight depression is dealing with what I think and what I talk about. I have an accountability partner who knows everything there is to know about me. I tell that person what I am thinking and have given her permission to coach me to the next level. When I choose to talk about negative things, she rreminds me that I am going backwards. After years of allowing this accountability, I have also learned to ask her about issues I am thinking about. For instance if I have a negative thought about what someone has said to me, I simply ask her what she thinks the person may have meant by what she said. The first time I had the courage to question myself by asking my accountability partner what someone said I was so relieved to find out that what I was thinking wasn't what the person said to me. It is funny how the mind plays tricks on you. The Lord told me a long time ago that my thinking was upside down and backward. When a word spoken by someone reached my brain, somehow I turned it around and perverted it. Even a compliment given to a negative brain can be translated to be a negative.

The final thing and the most important course of treatment for my depression is to keep my relationship open to Jesus. Prayer and meditation have taught me the value of a sound mind. I quote the scripture from II Timothy 1:7 that God has not given us fear, but power, love and a sound mind as my mantra. During my healing Jesus has taught me some very special meditations that release negativity, teach me about His love and force wrong thoughts out of my mind. My daily walk with Jesus includes obedience, confession, and prayer about everything.

I do not claim to be an expert in depression for everybody, but this has been a long battle for me. I have become an expert on what keeps me from sinking into the depths of depression. I do not say this will work for everybody but it has worked for me and many others.

A note about a friend of mine. This friend came to me suffering from depression and addiction. She had a sack full of pills and a long list of doctors. I told her how Jesus had helped me. I told her about the three part plan He gave me for me. She had the medications, so I was sure with that I could help her. What I could add would work for her. Immediately, we scheduled her medicines to be taken on time. She was required to follow our program of going to bed at the same time each night. She had to get up at the same time each morning. She was to eat three meals a day which were nutritional. She was to walk, not forty five minutes at first, but to be outside for forty five minutes walking as long as she could. She was required to be in a social environment during the day and could only isolate in the evenings.

After a week I noticed a marked improvement. She was laughing. She was walking. She was thinking more clearly but she wanted to go back to bed during the day. She did not want to help with any chores. After talking with her more than once, I realized that something was happening with her. She did not want to get better. She really didn't want the responsibility of life at all. Her body, soul and spirit were responding to the treatment, but she didn't want it. She went to her doctor and wanted him to change the way we did the program. He told her no. I really believe that he noticed a change in her for the better.

After all she was alert, articulate and physically looked better. She left the program after that. I have often wondered what happened to her. She was so desperate for help when she first arrived, but when the help was working, she had no excuse.

Our program is located across the street from the state mental health facility. After I had started walking and requiring our clients to walk and do other things that will help their brain repair I noticed that the facility across the street was implementing exercise into their program. I have also read much about the new mental health treatments for mental illnesses. All of the best ones implement healthy diet, exercise and spiritual meditation. The Amen Clinic, a well-known brain research clinic, uses all of the above treatments for depression. They go one step further and encourage professional counselors as part of a team to heal depression.

In conclusion, anger steals mercy from life. Anxiety replaces healthy fear and depression robs a person's joy. As anger comes under control, mercy returns. As anxiety is healed, a healthy reverence and awe returns to life. When depression subsides, joy becomes the driving force in a person's life. Nehemiah in chapter eight verse nine said the joy of the Lord is our strength. We can interpret that to mean having the Lord's joy gives us strength. His joy is being in fellowship with us. Jesus said for the joy that awaited Him He endured the cross. **Hebrews 12:2, "Looking unto Jesus the author and finisher of our faith; who for the joy that was set before him endured the cross, despising the shame, and is set down at the right hand of the throne of God."**

## Chapter 20

## Spiritual Aspects of Addiction

When women come to Bethesda House of Mercy there is at least a twofold reason. First they come to stop using drugs. That is the most evident reason. Each one has some inkling of hope that they can learn to live sober lives. The second reason they come to Bethesda is they are on a quest for God. These women all want to know who God is and how they can find Him. The problem comes when they fail to realize that addiction is a body, mind and soul or spirit issue. God himself is a triune God. He is three in one. He is Father, Son and Holy Spirit. A person cannot fully understand this concept but he or she must accept this truth by faith. Man is a triune man. He is body soul and spirit. Paul himself said, **"may the God of peace, sanctify you through and through. May your whole spirit, soul and body be kept blameless at the coming of our Lord Jesus Christ."** According to this verse, God wants to sanctify each of us through and through. The word sanctify just means to purify or to free from the guilt of sin, according to the Strong's Concordance reference number thirty seven.

The body is easily identified because the body is how one person identifies another. The body includes all the physical attributes of a person. The soul usually refers to the personality aspects of a person. This personality is made up of the mind, the will and the emotions. The spirit, that is the human spirit, is the part of mankind which is formed first and includes all the basic instincts of man including the drive to survive, the drive to know his creator and the drive to be independent.  One example of the distinction of the trinity of man is a man in a coma.  The body is present, the spirit is present but the soul or personality is not present.  The spirit leaves the body when the body dies, but the soul can die long before the spirit leaves.

Addiction, we have seen, touches the physical body and it touches the personality or emotions and will of a person.  Without a doubt, addiction touches the spirit of man.

The body of a person relates to the world at large.  The body touches the environment and the environment touches the body.  The soul of a person relates to other people.  The soul touches other people and other people touch the soul of man.  The spirit of a person, the human spirit, is where God touches man and where man touches God.  The scriptures say that we were dead in our trespasses and sin.  The body was not dead, the soul was not dead, but the spirit was dead.  When God touches man his human spirit is then made alive in Christ.

Let me say without any reservation that God is God and He can do whatever He wants to do.  He can if He so chooses reach down and zap a person and in a moment the person can be changed in body, soul and spirit.  But that usually doesn't happen.

What has usually happened in the lives of those I have worked with is that God touches the spirit making it alive and then the spirit affects the soul which in turn affects the body. I have seen it work like this: A person meets God and his or her spirit is made alive to the new life. The spirit begins to be fed with the word of God for changing behaviors and the soul is affected. The soul is affected first by the way it thinks and then by the decisions made and finally by the way the feelings react. The body follows with a new way to do things. The spirit brings life, personality refined, and those things work out into the hands and feet. The hands become helpers and the feet take the body to new places.

Let's go back to the addicted person looking for God. The mind is a negative place in the life of an addict. The mind of an addict is twisted to believe the only thing in life that is worthwhile is the drug of choice. The human spirit is wrecked. The addict's human spirit has little or no concept of the true and living God. The only god that it knows is the drug of choice. The false god of drugs has set itself up in the human spirit as "one that can help the addict." Since the human spirit has accepted that false god, the god has been able to make its way into the personality of the person. The drug of choice helps the person think, make decisions and tells the addict how to feel. With those things in place the body follows. The hands become weapons by hitting, stealing, and slapping.

The feet become transportation to wrong and deadly places.

In my opinion this is why we have so many who have "jail house religion." This is a term used for those who go to jail and seek Jesus, and seem to be really changed, only to get out of jail and "lose" everything. When the spirit is made alive in Christ the war starts in the spirit of the man or woman for total control. Before the "new birth" (which by the way is spiritual) the dominating principality or the king of the person was drugs. That "drug lord" has set up his kingdom in the spirit of the person. The "drug lord" of the person is not very happy to give up his rule and reign, so to speak.

That "drug lord" has lost his authority in the spirit of the man when Jesus comes in to the spirit. Scriptures tell us about someone who is stronger and able to overcome the strongman. **Matthew 12:29 , "For who is powerful enough to enter the house of a strong man like Satan and plunder his goods? Only someone even stronger-- someone who could tie him up and then plunder his house."**

Since addiction is so insidious and baffling and cunning, if the "drug lord" is not able to be king in the spirit after salvation he will take up lordship in the soul and the body. Let's think about that for a moment. How confusing it is to see someone who one day "gets saved" and wants to be sober and the next day is out doing drugs again. If it is confusing for you, the one looking at it from the outside, how much more confusing is it for the person who is actually doing drugs?

Instead of reaching out to the addict to help him or her get the "drug lord" out of his soul and body through spiritual growth and maturity, the church or other Christians will often toss the person aside as a fake. Now the addict, confused about what has happened, is rejected by the very people who should be able to help him or her. With no church the addict continues to surrender his mind, will and emotions (soul) over to the "drug lord." But what so many have told me is they are more confused and more unhappy and now the drugs do not really work as well as they should. The human spirit which once was friends with the soul and body is now at war. This is what Paul calls the war in his members.

If the spiritual battle which rages inside an addict is to be surrendered to Jesus, the addict must learn about the Christian disciplines and be helped to develop those disciplines.

The doctrine of addiction is a primary spiritual problem. The desperate need today is for a sober people.

Disciplines are a useful tool to get us in touch with God so that He can make the necessary changes in our life.

Meditation is to faith as worry is to fear. Meditation fuels faith while worry fuels fear. Someone has said that if you can worry you know how to meditate. Worry focuses on the negative aspects of life while meditation focuses on the word of God. Addicts must learn to meditate on the word of God. **Joshua 1:8, "This book of the law shall not depart out of thy mouth; but thou shalt meditate therein day and night, that thou mayest observe to do according to all that is written therein: for then thou shalt make thy way prosperous, and then thou shalt have good success."**

When a person meditates on the word of God, changes for the good begin to happen. The word of God is powerful and is able to bring a person to repentance of sin and direct a person to obedience. Suppose a person begins to meditate on "Thou shalt not steal," one of the Ten Commandments. The more a person meditates on the word, the more it becomes a part of himself. The spirit of God which is now alive in the person begins to work the word into the soul of that person. He is not only thinking about it, but he is able to make decisions based on that word. His feelings begin to change about stealing and therefore his body is not running to steal, and his hands now are working for things instead of stealing them. Thus the discipline of meditation has become spiritual and has changed a person's life.

Prayer is talking to God. If a person stops to think about praying as having a conversation with God the almighty that could be a life changing event. To have a conversation with the creator is very humbling. The bible says that God bends down to listen.

Can you imagine that? He, meaning God, bends down to hear us. WOW! Does that not just kink every brain transmitter you have? To think that the creator of the universe takes the time and effort to bend down and listen to us blows my circuits yet that is what the psalmist envisioned as he wrote the scriptures. In Psalm 116:2 the writer said "Because He bends down to listen I will pray as long as I have breath." (NLT)

So often we picture God as austere and unapproachable but the psalmist gives another side to Him. In my mind's eye I see God lower Himself from the proverbial waist and tilting His head towards the earth to hear a whispered prayer from me. Would God really want to hear from me or you? YES! YES! YES!

One of my friends can't understand a personal relationship with an omnipotent God. He thinks that because we are in the flesh that God cannot be personal with us and converse with us. But this scripture makes me believe that God is trying His best to have a relationship with us. That may be illogical or even unbelievable to some, but that relationship is what keeps me going when things get rough or even when things are going smoothly. That one scripture is pretty hopeful, don't you think?

I have a sort of dare for you who are having trouble believing in a God who cares about you. Take a few minutes and let your mind just begin to picture the most amazing person you can think of taking time and bending down to hear a child. Then transfer that to thinking that Jesus, who is in heaven, is bending down to hear you today. If you dare imagine and begin to hope, Jesus will become personal to you and you will be forever changed.

Study is a discipline. A person can study a book, the Bible or a subject. To study as a discipline means more. A person must learn to study life. He or she must do contemplative study of his own life and life as it exists outside him. Study on this level is more than repetition or concentration. It is more about comprehension and reflection. Imagine how addiction would change if an addict could and would learn to reflect on where he or she is in life and where he or she is going in life. Imagine the changes that would be made if an addict would learn to comprehend the gravity of addiction and the part it plays in shaping the lives of those around him or her.

Paying attention to nature, to people, to what is going on around a person helps that person learn what controls a person. An addict learning the Christian discipline of study must learn to ask questions.

Fasting is a discipline. Fasting food is the typical biblical fast. An addict must discover how the body chemistry works before attempting a spiritual fast because feeling hunger can trigger a relapse. Fasting is done to grow closer to God, so an addict can determine to fast drugs and alcohol until he or she gets a more intimate relationship to God to give them up completely. As in any fast one should pay close attention to the attitude of the heart.

God intended man to be simple. Simplicity is an inward decision that results in an outward manifestation. In other words, you decide to simplify your life and then your life becomes simple in terms of having things and doing things. The simple life is the focused life. When an addict simplifies his or her life, there is no duplicity. The addict gives up being one way in front of sober people and the other way in front of people using drugs.

The fact that a person is living without things is not a true sign that the person is living in simplicity. Economics is not a true indicator of simplicity. Poverty is not an indicator of simplicity. Poor people may have modest or simple circumstances but may not be satisfied with what they have. They may desire more and more but never be satisfied. Satisfaction is the only true sign of simplicity. Those living in simplicity have things because they provide a service or they benefit the kingdom of God. They do not desire things for the sake of having things.

Solitude is different than loneliness. For the addict loneliness is almost impossible to handle. But solitude, the ability to be alone and enjoy it, is a discipline that every addict should learn. Jesus becomes our best friend and then we have inward solitude and we lose the fear of being alone.

Many miss the mark by being silent when they should speak out. Many others miss the mark by speaking when they should be silent. As a person learns solitude, compassion for others grows.

The Bible teaches self-denial, not self-hatred. Addicts need to learn this lesson, since most have it backwards. They hate themselves but are self-indulgent. Addicts, along with most of the rest of the world, need to learn that they will not die if they don't get what they want.

In learning the discipline of Christian submission, the only limitations are when submission becomes destructive. Jesus taught revolutionary ideas when it comes to submission.

Service comes in two distinct categories. One is self-righteous service which tends to be only through human effort and requires external rewards. It is temporary and insensitive. This type of self-righteous service fractures the community it serves. True service comes from an intimate relationship with God. In this type of service the servant has a hard time telling the big from the small service. This type of servant serves because there is a need without a reward and doesn't care if anyone knows that he or she is serving. This type of service is a lifestyle.

The addict needs a place to confess. For confession to be authentic, there must be a mutual feeling of honesty and respect. The church should provide this place. **James 5:16 says "Confess your faults one to another that you may be healed."**

Guidance is yet another problem area for the addict. Will somebody step up to guide the addict into a sober lifestyle?

For the addict, celebration means "partying" to enjoy life. Addicts have to learn how to enjoy life without using. They cannot do this alone. Addicts need to experience laughter, they must learn that laughter brings more laughter. Joy is a conscious decision to view life in a positive way. Addicts must learn this in a corporate setting.

In the recovery world there is a phrase that says "one day at a time." Almost everybody uses it to get through the day, not making any promises to what tomorrow will bring. Without a doubt one day at a time is all we have to work with. But, do we use the slogan as a pathway to fail to commit? I have decided to change this slogan for myself to be "one day at a time with a lifetime commitment." It is like being married, we are married one day at a time but better not forget the life time commitment or you will find yourself in a world of trouble. One day at a time with a lifetime commitment changes everything for me. It says that though I must get through this day with change, my mind is made up and committed to real, lasting change. Many say about strong habitual practices that no one can commit to lasting change. I find that to be a copout. If lasting change is to occur, there has to be a mind transformation and a heart transplant. A new heart must be dedicated to new things, a strong commitment to a new life. Many enter the recovery world wanting their old life back, but that is never going to happen. They must get a new life, thus a lifetime commitment to something different. The heart is the seat of our desires, hopes, and dreams. Again, like getting married, a person doesn't go into a marriage contract with a hope that it will not last; their dream, their hope, their desire is for a lifetime commitment. This commitment is secured by one day at a time and doing the next right thing.

## Chapter 21

## "The Sickness"

Audrey's husband first contacted me about her alcohol use. She was married to a pastor and had the world by the tail. The family lived in a house built with her money, since she had worked in a highly lucrative industry. He pastored in a well-respected resort town in an old established church. Financially they were set. Physically they were beautiful. Nothing was missing in their world, well, except peace.

She was "pretty sick," he said. Pretty sick meant that she was no longer able to maintain household chores and her job was requiring treatment, or else. It was apparent that her husband would like to keep "it" quiet, that is why he brought her to us. The other reason was he didn't have insurance to cover a lengthy stay in a hospital. He wanted her to have spiritual help.

Her smile was infectious. Her personality was troubling. Not that she had a bad personality, that was not the problem. It was that she repeated her stories over and over. The stories of her life are what she repeated. I remember talking to her about the alcohol problem and it was like she didn't or couldn't understand what I would say to her.

This type of conversation is not unusual because alcoholics live in denial. But, there was something more. Audrey completed her ninety days and then she went home. Her husband hoped she would return to work, but that didn't happen. Her short term memory was totally gone.

A couple of years passed and her husband called me again. This time she was very, very sick. Her diagnosis was grim. The alcohol had caused senile dementia which to the untrained eye appeared to be early onset Alzheimer's. She walked with a stumbling gait and her short term memory was completely gone. What she could remember she talked about like it was yesterday. She spoke of being pregnant which was at least sixteen years prior. She spoke of her once successful career as though she had worked yesterday.

She could not remember that alcohol was bad for you. She had to be kept far away from alcohol of any kind. She was forty nine years old but alcohol had taken her life, though she didn't die until she was fifty four.

I guess the saddest part of this story is the way the other women in addiction treated Audrey. Even though they were told that she was a victim of alcoholism, they believed she could be "saved." These women tried everything to "save" her. They would argue with her and demand that she listen to them. Audrey said that she would change, but the next day it was all the same. She would ask the same questions over and over day after day after day. We put signs up to remind her not to rake leaves in the rain. Her mind was prone to compulsive acts and she had raked her yards as a child and now in order for her to think she was helping, she had to rake yards. The weather was terrible one day and I looked out the window to see Audrey drenched from head to toe raking leaves. "Come inside," I said as I led her into the house. She said, "I need to rake these leaves. I don't know where they come from."

Finally, Audrey began to get hostile and the women were hostile to her so she had to leave Bethesda. She was placed in a personal care home where she died about two years later. I went by to see her from time to time, but she didn't remember me. My heart was broken. She is a real life example of what excessive alcohol can do to the brain. You might not believe the reports of science or medicine until you live with an Audrey.

Virginia was in her early thirties when she came to Bethesda. Her mother was just so grateful that she had someplace to go. This was another case in which the addicted women did not believe what was happening to this woman. She seemed sober when she arrived. Her mother did say that she had been drinking. I cautioned them both that alcohol can be dangerous to detox from without medical help. They both agreed that she had been "through it" many times and so they signed off on the medical release.

We had planned a baptism service on the night she arrived. The entire group of women always travel with me since the ministry is a family style ministry. Before the baptism started, Virginia started to mumble under her breath. She then got louder and louder. All at once she began cursing as loud as she could. The group with us and those at the church were stunned.

She was slipping into a fantasy world or delirium caused by the alcohol leaving her body. By the grace of God and some good training, I was able to calm her down, but not until she ran out of the church and started down the roadway.

Later that night she began hallucinating, telling the girls that her daddy was downstairs waiting on her to come to him. She was a wreck. After a few days, she finally came to her senses and began to get her sanity back.

One of the other women in the program came to me to tell that "she was faking." I explained that Virginia wasn't faking anything. She was in psychosis from drinking too much alcohol. When the alcohol began to leave her brain, she was confused. But the other woman could not believe it. But, you see, I could believe it because I was the one to calm her down. I prayed earnestly that her mind would return to her. I am not sure how sane she was after that because when the "miseries" set in she convinced herself that she could return home and remain sober. The last I heard, she was drinking again.

It took about three years for one of our clients to return to sanity. She had auditory and visual hallucinations for about a year after she stopped using drugs. She would say, "Do you hear them? The drugs are calling me to come to them." I asked an addiction counselor what was happening to her. She told me cocaine psychosis. She told me to pray that she would come back to her senses, because sometimes they remain like that until they die.

The greatest way to stop drugs is to never start. There are not promises that once a person starts that their brain will return to its intended state. Addiction is a sin that can take you farther than you want to go and keep you longer than you want to stay.

Two things about these particular stories stand out. One is that the other women didn't believe what was happening and the women who suffered from the debilitations could not get better. One group could not stand to look in a mirror that reflected what drugs or alcohol can really do to the brain. The other group crossed a line and could not return. We teach that there is always another relapse in every person, but there may not be another recovery.

## Chapter 22

## Breathing Clean Air

Waking up on dry land was a shock to my system. Recovery began but restoration was and is a process. I had loving arms to embrace me with warmth so the shock would not be permanent. Listening ears and withheld judgments placed me in a safe place to heal. My watery grave which had become my bathing pool was gone. It seemed odd at first to breathe without struggling.

Now I know that sounds weird to you guys who have never almost drowned. But if you have ever drowned on dry earth, you know what I mean. It gets pretty comfortable in the bath. It is like a frog in boiling water, once the frog is allowed to warm with the water, he thinks that the water is safe. So it is with life's hardest issues.

I've been breathing on dry earth for about twenty years or more. Sometimes on the rainy afternoons or the cold grey days I look back to the water bath. It is then that I remind myself that the watery grave is really a watery grave and not a warm bath. I tell myself the past is past and the now is all that matters.

The truth is that once you have been in that warm water, the memory, the thought is planted and you have to stay far away from the thoughts.

I learned that to breathe is to breathe in life. To breathe is to inhale God. He provides the air, I provide the lungs. So I just breathe. At first it was a gasp. Many days I tried not to breathe, but my lungs screamed for air. Then I would force too much air into my lungs thinking more is better. Finally through all the stages of restoration I have described in the 12 Gates of Recovery and Restoration I could breathe in rhythm and without a struggle. I encourage you to learn to breathe. Maybe you will begin today. Go ahead take a breath.

www.ingramcontent.com/pod-product-compliance
Lightning Source LLC
Chambersburg PA
CBHW071118090426
42736CB00012B/1947